"A grand book of Moon myths and ta
This book should prove to be a fascinating read for adults and chil-
dren alike."

—D.J. Conway
author, *Moon Magick*

AWAKEN THE MOON-STRUCK WONDER IN YOU

For those who hunger for the celebrations of nature as practiced long ago, here is your invitation to begin again. Never
before have the many faces of the Moon been seen in a single volume directed to those who can truly appreciate its
eternal position in our lives.

The tales in *Moonlore* are not confined by geographical or
cultural boundaries. They are tales and legends that the
elders of ancient and more recent societies have carried
through the generations. There are legends dedicated to
the time that each Moon rides the sky. There are tales of
gods and goddesses that rule the "evening sun" and tales
that speak of virtue, danger, mystery and magic.

The lore of different cultures often distinguishes one
group of people from the next. Yet, in compiling the mythology of the Moon, the overall effect seems to bind, rather
than separate, the people on Earth. This classic collection of
folk tales is a celebration of the rising of the Moon, when all
peoples of all lands become of single heart.

There is a universal bond of brotherhood and sisterhood
in the celebration of our Moon. It is this lunar bond that
transcends time and place and serves ultimately to affirm
our connection in the universe.

ABOUT THE AUTHOR

Gwydion O'Hara is dedicated to the research, study, and practice of ancient folkways that survive today. For more than twenty years, he has looked for the practices of the people of the land, wherever they could be found and in whatever aspect they would present themselves. His studies have brought him in contact with others who hold a common respect for the old ways, offering the opportunity to watch and work with different groups in both the United States and Canada. In his studies, he has pursued the areas of herbology, mythology, folklore, and folk magic. He gained recognition in New York and Toronto as a competent tarot reader and lectured on the subject for the Toronto Psychic Society. A love for the lore of the simple folk, however, always has been behind his work. *Moonlore* is a product of that devotion.

To Write to the Author

If you wish to contact the author or would like more information about this book, please write to the author in care of Llewellyn Worldwide and we will forward your request. Both the author and publisher appreciate hearing from you and learning of your enjoyment of this book and how it has helped you. Llewellyn Worldwide cannot guarantee that every letter written to the author can be answered, but all will be forwarded. Please write to:

Gwydion O'Hara
℅ Llewellyn Worldwide
P.O. Box 64383-342-5, St. Paul, MN 55164-0383,
U.S.A.

Please enclose a self-addressed, stamped envelope or $1.00 to cover costs. If outside the U.S.A., enclose an international postal reply coupon.

Free Catalog from Llewellyn

For more than 90 years Llewellyn has brought its readers knowledge in the fields of metaphysics and human potential. Learn about the newest books in spiritual guidance, natural healing, astrology, occult philosophy, and more. Enjoy book reviews, New Age articles, a calendar of events, plus current advertised products and services. To get your free copy of *Llewellyn's New Worlds of Mind and Spirit*, send your name and address to:

Llewellyn's New Worlds of Mind and Spirit
P.O. Box 64383-342-5, St. Paul, MN 55164-0383, U.S.A.

Moonlore

Myths and Folklore from Around the World

Gwydion O'Hara

1996
Llewellyn Publications
St. Paul, Minnesota 55164-0383, U.S.A.

Cover design: Tom Grewe
Cover art: Beth Wright
Interior illustrations: Robin Larsen
Book design and layout: Ronna Hammer
Editor: Rosemary Wallner
Project coordinators: Pamela Henkel and Jessica Thoreson

Library of Congress Cataloging-in-Publication Data

O'Hara, Gwydion.
    Moonlore: myths and folklore from around the world / Gwydion O'Hara– 1st ed.
        p.   cm.
    Includes bibliographical references and index.
    ISBN 1-56718-342-5 (pbk.)
    1. Moon–Religious aspects. 2. Moon–Mythology. I. Title.
    BL325.M56034   1996
    292.2'12–dc20   95-51456
                                                                          CIP

Llewellyn Publications
A Division of Llewellyn Worldwide, Ltd.
P.O. Box 64383, St. Paul, MN 55164-0383

To those, past and present, who glory in the ever-changing constancy of the Moon.

Contents

PART 2: LUNAR DIGNITARIES

PART 3: MORE MOON TALES

Preface

I offer this volume as one of the few of its kind. It is, without doubt, unique in its specific nature.

I wrote the first draft of *Moonlore* in Toronto over ten years ago. That manuscript was the result of many long hours of research and very much the labour of love that artists and writers dream about—thoughts seem to flow easily when they come from the heart. This book's origin is worth mentioning because the writing style retains some of the flavour of Canada. This style is especially apparent in the British/Canadian spellings I use throughout.

Although I have dedicated sections to each traditional Moon, *Moonlore* spans both time and culture—I have included bits of the old and new. Some of the legends are what remains from ancient days. Some are taken from newer cultures. I am pleased to include the legends of tiny South Pacific Island cultures as well as the mythology of the classical Romans and Greeks. Though the tribes may speak in different tongues and tell each tale in a different way, all have fallen under the spell of their own Moon dreams.

Acknowledgments

Although *Moonlore* was originally undertaken as a solitary effort, this book could never have reached completion without the help of others. In particular, I thank Mattea for helping to create the quiet haven away from the demands of everyday obligations and distractions—a special place carved out of time and space in which this writing was made possible. I also recognize Ann for providing the physical means to complete this offering, and Tamarra for the never-ending inspiration that arises from our special bond.

Introduction

Since the earliest human age, before the rise of even the most ancient beginnings of civilization, humans have had an innate need for stability. The greatest threat posed to the stability and day-to-day survival of humans was at the hands of nature.

The harsh elements of nature's cycles were the greatest obstacle to existence. Humans realized that their very life depended on the mercy of this most powerful adversary. Early humans knew that their emergence through the difficult conditions in which they found themselves would have to be trusted to the whims of nature.

Living in such dark and dangerous times, the search for something constant was inevitable. To find something stable—something that could offer hope in a changing young world full of new dangers at every turn—would be a monumental undertaking.

In this quest, nature, the greatest enemy, also becomes the greatest friend. As humans turned to the natural order in search of hope, they quickly realized that nature was not only a divine ally but also the fulfillment of their search. The Moon, one of the many mysteries of nature, held special significance.

When the sky blackened and the world turned cold, humans could depend on the light of the Moon to cast its radiance. If the search for food was unsuccessful and the weather severe, the regular waxing and waning cycles of the Moon could restore hope.

In time, this heavenly messenger—which unceasingly gave renewal to the spirit and enough encouragement to face the elements of destruction with new life—was deified. Humans honoured, adored, and worshipped the Moon. As they paid more attention to the Moon, they saw it as a heavenly reflection of their life upon the earth. Farmers could plant crops according to the cycles of the Moon. When the appropriate Moon of the year appeared in the sky, hunters knew their season had begun.

In cultures around the world, the Moon became a goddess or god—and a symbol of its deity. Each year's Moons were given names by which their pagan worshippers might know them. In the night sky, the earliest humans found their deity, their almanac, and their guide to life. Through tradition and legend, nature's children throughout the world have carried down these ideas to modern times.

Moonlore is a collection of the tales and legends that the elders of ancient and more recent societies have passed down through the generations. You'll find legends dedicated to the time of night when each particular Moon rides the sky. You'll read tales of the gods and goddesses who ruled the evening sun; and tales that speak of the virtue, danger, mystery, and magic embodied in the Moon.

Enjoy *Moonlore* as well as learn from it; the tales will speak to your emotions as well as your intellect. Through the dreamer within—or through the invisible bonds that tie the hearts of modern people to the hearts of ancestors of ages passed—you will awaken your own moonstruck, childlike wonder.

PART 1:
A Moon in Every Month

A Window into the Past

*T*hrough the generations, people have handed down folktales and legends to delight imaginations and inspire dreamers. Within the ancient cultures from which we inherited these marvelous tales, however, was a much greater significance to the world of fantasy, magic, and mythology. Those who preserved these lunar sagas through written and verbal tradition did not merely pass on nice old stories; these people left a legacy that offers a window into the past. They have, in the guise of imaginative narratives, given us a glimpse of the way they lived.

Each month when the Moon rose full over the lands, those who farmed, tended livestock, and followed animals in the hunt knew her by a different name. The names they chose for the midnight sun often reflected what was important in their lives at the time each Moon ascended. At planting time, the lunar cycle that watched over the earth's activities was known as the Seed Moon, the Planter's Moon, or the Sprouting Grass Moon. When the time for crop gathering was upon them, the people who worked the land saw the Harvest Moon, the Barley Moon, or the Big

Feast Moon rise above them. When harvest time was done and people turned to the hunt for their main food source, the Blood Moon, the Hunter's Moon, or the Killing Deer Moon ascended.

Sometimes, lunar cycle names reflected the Moon's mythology and folk legends. The Hare Moon, the Wolf Moon, and the Sun House Moon are some of the names that may be rooted in folktales.

Lunar names can also reflect the customs and traditions of a particular culture. We still recall the Play Moon, the Running Season Moon, and the Hoop and Stick Game Moon.

Finally, there are the Moons of transition. The original Moon children were people of the land. They depended on the natural order for their survival, and they looked to the natural wonders with awe and reverence. They were the *paganis*, the pagans, and the people of the heaths, the heathens. With the march of time, many who revered the lunar cycles were converted to Christianity. Although their careful monitoring of the lunar phases and cycles was firmly rooted in tradition, the names changed to reflect a newly adopted belief system. This was the advent of the Christmas Moon, Easter Moon, and Christ's Moon.

Lunar names span several cultures and stretch far back into time. Those used in this book are the ones learned through verbal tradition. Originally, their roots were in European tradition. Many of the Saxon names for the lunar cycles are the same as those presented here. There seems, however, to be some influence from North American Indian lore. Some of the lunar names as presented in this offering are very close to those that survive in tribal legendry.

Wolf Moon

January's Moon is traditionally known as the Wolf Moon. Although some of the Moon cycles are known by the same names through different cultural traditions and folklore, the name Ice Moon is another name commonly used for the first Moon of the year.

Today, people throughout the world mark time on the same calendar; January is the beginning of the year. In the natural world, however, January is the middle of the winter season, a time of death and desolation. It is appropriate, therefore, that the legends chosen for the Wolf Moon are tales of both beginnings and endings.

The Wolves of Ironwood

SCANDINAVIA

In the beginning of time, an endless abyss known as Ginnungagap existed. From out of this abyss the first worlds formed. To the north, the icy world of Niflheim was formed. To the south was the fire world of Muspelheim, home of Surtur, the fire-giant. Between these worlds was Midgard, the world of humans.

The great giant Ymir was born of the ice melting from the streams of Niflheim and sparks of fire from Muspelheim. As the giant slept, frost giants were

formed from Ymir's feet. From his left armpit, the giant Buri was created.

Buri was wed to Bestla, the daughter Balthor, one of the frost giants. In time, three sons were born of their union. These were the first of the Norse gods, called Vili, Ve, and Odin, the chief of the gods.

Odin and his brothers grew to hate Ymir and the frost giants. They attacked and killed Ymir. When he died, his blood flooded the lands and drowned all the frost giants but two.

The three brothers formed the world from the body of the slain giant. They made the seas, mountains, and forest lands. From two fallen trees—an elm and an ash—they created the first man and woman and endowed them with the gifts of life, knowledge, and emotion.

The brother gods created the Sun, Moon, and Stars, and set them in their rightful places in the sky. Moon led the way and is forever pursued by Sun; the constant procession of night and day, day and night. This is how it began and this, according to the plan of the gods, was how it was meant to be for all time.

The new world of the three Norse gods was a wonderful creation. Only they were capable of such artistry. The world's completion was a monument to their honour.

A witch named Ironwood lived a life of darkness in the shadow of the trees. Perhaps she was jealous over the wonder of the gods' creation, or perhaps she merely had a sour disposition over the state of her own life—whatever the reason, Ironwood had other plans for Sun and Moon.

Ironwood bore two wolves—Hati Hrodvitnisson and Skoll—and set them in pursuit of the twin lights of night and day. The Moon never rests in her transit across the heavens and Hati Hrodvitnisson is never far behind, obsessed with the thought of devouring her light. The Sun follows, pursued by Skoll.

Occasionally, Hati Hrodvitnisson manages to take a bite out of the Moon. This is the phenomenon that we now know as the eclipse. The Norse people are at the ready when Hati Hrodvitnisson catches the Moon. They shout, beat pans together, and raise as loud a racket as they can until the Moon is restored to its fullness.

One day, however, the hunger of the twin wolves will be sated. They will succeed in devouring the Sun and Moon. Darkness will descend upon the earth and the time of Ragnorok, the Twilight of the Gods, will be upon us. It will be the beginning of the end. Until that time, though, the endless chase continues across the sky.

Wolf Spirit
Pawnee Native American Tribe

The Pawnee Indians are one of the most honoured tribes in North America. Their name is taken from the word pa'ni, which has been translated to mean wolf. This is, indeed, the tribe of the wolf. Their traditions, customs, and legendry herald the Wolf Spirit.

Tirawa, the Great Spirit, placed Wolf Spirit in the sky to watch out for Evening Star. Tirawa placed Wolf's animal brothers—Black Bear, Mountain Lion, and Wild-Cat—next to Wolf Spirit in attendance of the Moon.

Great was the power of Wolf Spirit and his fellows in their place in the sky. They came to be known as Black Star, Yellow Star, White Star, and Red Star. These Star Beasts sent animals like themselves to live upon the earth. These same animal spirits were responsible for many of the earth's creations. They sent autumn, spring, winter, and summer. They sent clouds, thunder, lightning, and wind. They sent the cottonwood, elm, willow, and box elder. They created the four kinds of corn—black, yellow, white, and red. And it was these great and powerful spirits that guarded Evening Star each night.

As great as these Star Warriors were, the power of Morning Star, the Sun, was greater. In time, the Sun vanquished Wolf Spirit and his brothers. In honour of their greatness, Morning Star set Wolf Spirit and the other Star Beasts to hold up the four quarters of the universe.

Wolf Spirit, once guardian of the Moon, now stands as devoted servant of the Sun. Yet his likeness upon the earth is still heard howling when Evening Star rises in the sky. Could it be that the creation of Wolf Spirit yet remembers the ancient ties to the Moon? The lone wolf singing his songs to the Moon is following the ways of his ancestors who first helped the Moon to ascend to her nightly station.

Storm Moon

The Moon of February is the Storm Moon. During this month, storms rage upon the earth and the winter months are still very much with us. The hardships that accompany the harsh weather present a daily challenge to the peoples of the earth. The waters rage in the form of snow and ice upon the land; they toss the ships upon the sea as if they were feathers in a wind.

Monsters of the Sicilian Sea
ANCIENT GREECE

*The ancient Greeks tell the story of Scylla and Charybdis, two clash-
ing rocks, which today are related to two rocky isles in the narrow
Strait of Messina in the Sicilian Sea. Scylla and Charybdis are symbolic of all the dangers of sea travel. They represent the tidal waves,
violent storms, and vulnerability of sailors who venture out into the
terrifying majesty of the waters.*

*The water is very much the domain of the Moon. The sailors of
past civilizations knew this well. Their modern-day descendants*

have documented the Moon in their books of science, noting the ebb and flow of the sea. Many of today's sailors, however, cannot recognize the dangers of the deep waters as their ancestors did. Fewer, still, remember their stories.

Charybdis was the daughter of Poseidon, the sea god. Her home was beneath a lone fig tree on a small island in a narrow stretch of sea highway. One day Zeus turned Charybdis into a whirlpool. Three times a day, she sucked in the seawater that surrounded her, including everything that ventured within the reach of her mighty currents. Many unwary sailors became her victims when she swallowed up their vessels as they passed through her domain.

Scylla was once a fair nymph. Circe, Mistress of the Moon and Sorceress of the Night, became enraged when the nymph became beloved of the sea-god on whom Circe had her own designs. The Moon Goddess worked her magic on the maid and turned Scylla into a sea demon.

Scylla became a terrifying creature with twelve feet and six long necks. At the end of each neck was a head endowed with a triple row of sharp teeth. Beneath the waves, in a dark cave set in an undersea cliff, the monster lay in wait for the sailors who travelled upon the waters. As an unsuspecting vessel passed above, Scylla swam up from her watery cave. Each of her heads would pick a sailor from the ship's deck and carry him beneath the waters. These sailors were never seen again.

The great hero Odysseus piloted his ship between Charybdis and Scylla. Through the able seamanship of a worthy captain, Odysseus evaded the currents of

Charybdis. However, as he sailed passed Scylla, the sea demon caught six of his crew from the deck of his vessel and devoured them.

These giants still stand, beckoning to unsuspecting sailors. Although time has made them less animated, experienced sailors are well aware that the dangers of the sea are not above the waters, but lurk silently beneath. The tidal wave that swallows villages, the whirlpool that devours ships, and the sea storms that violently shake the waters are not born of the surface waters. They find their beginnings in the dark depths of the Moon's mysterious waters, in the very bosom of the sea.

An Arctic Sea Demon

INUITS

The Alaskan Inuits know Igaluk, the Moon god, as the supreme deity in the universe. Under his watchful eye, the world's living creatures were created. Many versions of Igaluk's legends exist. Carried primarily through oral tradition, the remembrance of the tales has been less than precise. The tales still survive, however, coloured with the flavour of whatever storyteller last repeated the myth.

Sedna, often seen as a one-eyed sea goddess, may have been a child of Igaluk, the Moon god. Some say, though,

she was born of the union of Moon man and Sun woman; others say she was the daughter of the people of the earth.

Although the storytellers do not agree about her birth, they do agree that Sedna was a sinister demon. To look into her single eye was to invite death. Sedna despised the people of the earth. With evil eye and violent temper, it was only the *angokoq*, or tribal shaman, who dared approach her. She was the mistress of the dead and controlled the human population by drowning people in her storms.

According to one legend, Sedna began as a spiteful and unruly child. She ate any flesh she could find, with little regard to whose death was necessary to feed her carnal desires. One night, she began to eat the flesh of her father as he slept. Because of the horror of her behaviour, her father rowed her out to sea to throw her overboard.

But Sedna held fast to the side of the boat. Her father tried to loosen her grasp by hitting her hands with his paddle. Still, she held firmly. Finally, Sedna's father severed the girl's fingers, one by one. As each finger fell into the sea, it was transformed into a fish, whale, or seal. This was the beginning of those creatures that inhabit the sea.

Finally, Sedna sunk to the ocean bottom. She dwells there still, guarding the creatures of the waters. Despising people, she raises storms to prevent fishing. Because she is fingerless, she cannot comb the knots from her matted hair. Shamans visit her to ask her forgiveness and please her by brushing her hair. When the shaman is successful, Sedna holds back the storms and releases a few sea creatures to the shaman.

Chaste Moon

March's Moon is called the Chaste Moon. March is a time of purity. The earth has thawed and has loosened itself from the cold hands of winter. New life will soon emerge and the land will grow green with fertility. In March, however, the earth is but a child. What will develop into the ripened fruits of summer is yet young and innocent. It is the newborn babe; the youthful maiden yet untouched by love. In early spring, we celebrate the fleeting virtue of innocence. We see the certain potential of fruitfulness, yet give honour to the innocence of childhood as it is apparent in the maiden, and in this time upon the earth. This Moon and its legend are the reflection of the earth and its season.

Fana, the Chaste Maid

ANCIENT ROME

In a village lived Fana, a young maiden. She was an extraordinarily beautiful girl, with eyes as black as a raven and hair as soft as fine velvet.

She was not cradled in the lap of luxury but was of very modest and humble means. To satisfy her simple needs, she journeyed from one inn to another and performed whatever meager tasks that would earn her a hot meal and shelter from the night's cold winds. Sometimes, she roamed from farm to farm in search of

an honest day's work that might merit enough food to quiet her hunger and a warm place in the barn to sleep. Each new day found her renewing her tasks; and Fana gladly worked day and night to ensure her survival. She had no family and knew that her existence was solely dependent on the toil of her body given to a stranger with enough kindness to accept it.

Fana had few friends and remained alone—a stranger to the ways of love and caring. The only man to ever profess love to the peasant girl was an ugly, brutish fellow who could not distinguish the tenderness a true love might bring from his own crude feelings of passion. Fana saw the foul intent of his advances and could not bear even to look at him.

Late one evening, as Fana returned to the village from a farmhouse where she had been working, her beastly suitor jumped out in front of her from a thicket where he had hidden himself. Taking firm hold of the surprised maiden, the man cried out in delight, "You are mine, fair maid! There can be no escape. Even your cries will fade into the night unanswered and avail thee nought."

Fana stood motionless for a moment, frozen by her fear. She looked about her and saw no one who might come to her rescue. The words of victory from her assailant's mouth seemed, horribly, to be full of truth. Only the full Moon in the darkened sky above bore witness to her plight.

In desperation, Fana cast herself to her knees and cried, "I have no one on earth to protect my honour. Only thou, O Moon, can see me in my time of need. I do offer my solemn prayer to thee, O Lady of the

Midnight Skies. Thou art radiantly beautiful, flashing thy silver splendour over all the world. I pray that you cast your light upon the mind of this poor soul who would do his worst to me here. May he loosen his hold on me that I may continue my journey in the safety of your silver light."

When Fana's words were spoken, a form appeared before her, shadowy yet ever so bright. This lovely spirit of light spoke to the maid. "Rise up, girl, and get thee onward to thy journey's end," the spirit said. "Well hast thou earned my favour. No ruffian shall do thee harm as long as thou art in the silver shelter of my light. Thou art the purest creature upon the earth. In the days to come, thou shalt be one with my light. Thou shalt a goddess be, the Goddess of the Moon, the most radiant spirit of the innocence of life, and the Queen of all Enchantment, revered most highly among men."

Thus did it come to pass that Fana, the poor but honest peasant girl, became the spirit that dwells within the heart of nighttime's burning silver torch. Thus did Fana become the Goddess of the Moon.

The Reindeer Maid
CHUKCHI PEOPLE OF SIBERIA

The Moon descended from his place in the heavens to walk among the creatures of the earth in the form of a man. His visit was prompted by the beating of his lonely heart.

From his place in the sky, the Moon had seen a certain maiden. She was a young girl whose duty was to tend her father's herd of reindeer at night. She travelled away from her village to faithfully watch over the herd, alone but for the reindeer. She amused herself through the lonely nights by playing music on her flute.

The Moon had heard these sweet melodies many times as he sailed across the darkened sky. In fact, it was this sweet music that convinced the Moon that he must have the maid for his own. He wanted to take her back to the sky with him to live forever.

But as the innocent girl watched carefully over the herd, a wise old stag watched over her. The old stag saw the Moon man coming and hid the young girl by turning her into a lamp. Though the Moon left no part of the girl's tent unsearched, he could not find her.

Distressed, the Moon left the tent without his prize. As he left, however, the girl changed back to her youthful form and called out to the Moon, taunting him. He turned back to the tent and found it as he had before, empty but for a bed, blanket, and lamp.

As the Moon continued his search, he grew tired. He became pale and thin in his weakness until at last he was so thin that the girl was able to bind him up with a rope. He continued to grow weak and begged the girl for release.

At first, the maid refused to free her captive Moon. She was angry over his search for her. She was angry that he had wanted to carry her off to his home in the heavens without so much as asking her desires. Finally, the maid released the Moon and made him promise to attend his duties in the sky and never return to bother her again.

This the Moon has faithfully done. He remains in the sky, casting his bright light on the earth below. But perhaps his loneliness sometimes reminds him of his visit to the earth. When he remembers, the pain of his heart weakens his glow.

Seed Moon

April's Moon is called the Seed Moon. The equinox has already heralded the birth of spring, and the child earth is taking the first steps in its new life. It is a time of beginnings. The world is born anew and is filled with the fascination of the feeling of life that flows throughout its being. The child steps out into the light and begins to regard every wonderous miracle in the world, without and within.

Today, the wrinkled sages of the hills and farmlands, the wise old folk of the countryside, regard the Seed Moon as it rises in its season. As they gaze at the beautiful silver-blue torch in the nighttime sky, they quietly remember the tales of life, and the seeds of life the Moon both gives and protects.

The Seeds of the Aoa

SOUTH PACIFIC ISLANDS

Different ages and cultures have legends about the Moon's inhabitants. Different peoples recount the tales of the man, woman, toad, or hare that lives on the Moon. If we are to accept these ancient legends, we would have the Moon more heavily populated than some of our cities.

Along the landscape of the Pacific Islands, as far as one could see, was a beauty unrivalled anywhere in the world. Those who visited the South Pacific from foreign lands referred to this land as paradise. There was something divine about these islands that were rich with beauty.

Even in this land of enchantment, however, one sight was more wonderful than all the rest: a stately tree adorned with leaves of deep colour that shone with the lustre of moonlight. Every bough was heavily laden with green and yellow fruits. The natives knew this tree as Aoa. There was nothing more revered in all the land.

The sacred Aoa can no longer be found in the islands of the Pacific Ocean. Just what happened to endanger it has been forgotten. Some of the elders believe a succession of great tidal waves damaged it. Others believe a volcano that was thought to be extinct awoke with a sudden fury. Whatever the reason, the Aoa was in grave danger of succumbing to death. There seemed to be no hope for the most sacred and beautiful of trees.

Much of the sacred fruit lay on the ground, shaken from the boughs of the tree. As mere mortals, the natives knew there was little that they could do to prevent the disaster they saw unfolding before them. The elders decided to petition their gods for the salvation of the sacred Aoa. The elders prayed with all the strength and heart that was within them. They knew that time was not in their favour and hoped that the gods would be quick to heed their request.

Without warning, the heavens opened up and a hundred doves descended. The birds were bright and shining and wore feathers made of the sun's golden rays. Each flew to the place where the Aoa stood in peril. Each plucked a seed from the fallen fruit and turned back to the heavens. The golden doves made no

delay as they rose directly for the surface of the Moon. There, they let fall the sacred seeds.

The Aoa is lost to the earth, but the natives of the islands know that it will live forever under the protection of the Moon. In its home upon the lunar surface, it yet thrives from the seeds planted there so long ago by the golden flock of divine doves. Others may look at the dark spots on the Moon and see the man, woman, or beast of their own legends. In the South Pacific, the natives know that the dark spots are the great forests of Aoa trees that have sprung up from the sacred seeds.

$\mathcal{C}$hinese $\mathcal{S}$eed-$\mathcal{B}$irds

CHINA

Each child knows of the man in the Moon. According to Chinese legend, however, he did not always live upon the Evening Star. He was once a greedy neighbor.

Once there were two neighbors. One was a kind and gentle man, beloved of both human and beast. The other was a jealous, greedy man. So compassionate was the kind man that, when he found a bird with a broken wing, he not only helped to mend the wing but also kept the bird under his care until it was well enough to fly again.

When the bird was healed, the kind man released it to its home in the air. Grateful for the tender care, the bird dropped a magic seed in the gentle man's hand and told him to plant it. The man did as he was instructed. When he did, a green vine sprung from the seed. It was large and beautiful and heavily laden with ripe luscious fruit.

The kind man's jealous neighbor heard the tale of the magical seed. Thinking that he too might prosper from the bird's magic, he went into the woods. Finding a bird, the greedy neighbor broke the creature's wing. He then cared for the creature until the wing was healed.

As with the good neighbor, this man was also rewarded with a seed and given instructions to plant it. But the planted seed did not grow along the ground like a common vine. This magical growth grew straight up into the air, farther than anyone could see.

The greedy neighbor, anxious to gain his reward from the magic vine, climbed straight up the vine into the sky. When he reached the top, he found that he was standing upon the Moon and the vine had disappeared behind him. This unfortunate soul can still be seen upon the face of the Moon.

Hare Moon

The Moon of May is called the Hare Moon. May is rebirth of life upon the earth. With its reputation for being prolific, no creature is more suited than the hare as this month's symbol.

In researching legends for mythology appropriate to May's lunar cycle, there was no shortage of tales. Being a creature sacred to many of the lunar deities and of significant importance in many cultures, the legends regarding the hare seem to be as prolific as its reputation.

A Hare in the Moon

In the old days, a hare, a monkey, a fox, and a coot (water bird) became hermits. They lived in the wilderness and swore never to take the life of any living creature. The god Sakkira heard these creatures. He decided to test the strength of their vows and the depth of their faith.

Sakkira took upon himself the form of a brahmin (priest). Appearing before the monkey, he begged alms of him. The monkey set out at once and soon returned

with his arms heavily laden with mangoes. Sakkira accepted this gift with the humility of his assumed character and went on his way.

The brahmin next sought out the coot. When he found the hermit coot, he made the same request as he had to the monkey. In reply, the coot went to the river's edge. There, he found some fish lying on the ground, apparently forgotten by some fisherman. The coot gathered up the fish and returned to the brahmin. The coot presented his find to the holy man as his offering.

Next, the brahmin approached the fox and made a request for alms. The fox set out to find some food that he might offer to the priest. He returned with a pot of milk and a parcel of rice, which he had found on a plain, neglected by some shepherd. He presented his gift devoutly to the holy man.

At last, Sakkira came upon the hare. He again requested an offering. "Would that I could offer something to you, most noble priest," said the hare, "but I partake, myself, only of grass. Surely, this could be of no use to you."

Not to be thwarted in his testing of the hermit hare, Sakkira replied, "My friend, if you are a true hermit, you might offer me your own flesh in the hope of a future happiness."

"Your request is granted," said the hare, without a moment's hesitation. "You may do as you wish with this mortal shell." The brahmin, however, was not convinced of the hare's sincerity.

"Since you are willing to grant what I ask," said the brahmin, "I shall kindle a fire at the foot of the large rock. If you were to climb up on the rock, you could cast yourself into the flames. This would save me the trouble of first killing you and then dressing your flesh."

This request, too, was readily agreed to by the hare. While Sakkira kindled a fire, the hare climbed to the top of the rock. When the flames had reached a respectable height, the hare threw himself from the rock and headed into the hot flames. Before he could reach the burning fire, however, the flames disappeared and the brahmin assumed the shape of the god Sakkira.

Sakkira took the hare in his arms and traced his figure upon the surface of the Moon, so that every living creature in every part of the world could see it.

Even today, this figure of the hare is visible upon the face of the Moon. Many are like the monkey, the coot, and the fox, who offer to their gods that of little consequence, that which costs them nothing. A creature of the hare's faith, however, is a rare one. Sakkira's message is that whoever gives truly of themselves shall shine in glory with the brightness of the Moon for all time, even as the noble hare shines yet.

The Origin of the Harelip

HOTTENTOT PEOPLE OF SOUTH AFRICA

The time came when a decision had to be made regarding the fate of humans. Time had withered their bodies and the fullness of their existence had begun to decline. As it happened, the task of this most serious deliberation fell to the Moon.

The decision would be final and unchangeable. The judgement would have to be of great wisdom, for it would endure until the end of time. The Moon knew well the gravity of her task and did not enter into it lightly.

After much thought and consultation with the other gods of the old days, the fate of humans was decided. Just as it is with her own waxing and waning, it would be with humans. Men and women would rise to the fullness of their lives and then begin to die away. And just as the Moon, humans, after their deaths, would rise again with life renewed.

The Moon was pleased with her decision. It would mean that for all time humans would share her gift of renewal. Those of the earth below, she thought, should be the first to know how it shall be among them. She sent the hare with the news of her decision.

When the hare arrived upon the earth, all the men and women were busy with the work of preparation for the winter months. They stored what food and grain they had, wove fibers together to keep them warm, and strengthened their homes against winter's harsh winds.

So devoted to their work were they, in fact, that they did not even notice the arrival of the Moon's courier. The hare was upset over his apparent neglect. This, he thought, is surely no way to treat one of divine grace. He decided that the creatures of this mortal realm should be taught a lesson so that they would keep better manners in the days to come. The hare knew just the way to do it, too.

When at last he managed to get the attention of the people of earth, the hare told them that he had come carrying a most important message from the Moon. He told them that the fate of humanity, after much consideration, had been decided upon, and that he had been sent to deliver the news of the outcome.

The hare watched as the many assembled before him grew silent and waited anxiously to hear of their fate. At last, he arrived at the fulfillment of his purpose in descending to the earth. He began to deliver the message that he had brought, but the message he gave was not the one with which he had been sent.

"People of the earth," the hare began, "you can look into the darkness of the heavens at night and see the cycles of the divine Moon. She rises to the fullness of life and glory. Then she dies away and there is darkness. By her divine power, you can see her then rise yet again. Her power is the gift of renewal. Surely it is a gift devoutly to be wished even among the races of mortals. But it is a power that is truly divine. It could come only as a gift unto humans, for you are not of the holy realm. So watch the Moon as she transcends both life and death in her travels across the sky, and know that in her cycles is proof of the glory of those who inhabit the heavens. Like the Moon, those of the earth shall evermore grow to the fullness of their lives ere they begin to fade away. But to keep you ever aware that you are not of the same substance as those who dwell above, humans shall fade and rise again no more!"

With this, the hare took speedy leave of the earth and returned to the Moon, confident that he would never again descend to the earth unnoticed.

The Moon asked the hare how the humans reacted to the decision of the Moon to bestow the gift of renewal upon them. The hare, aware that he had disobeyed the command of his mistress, was reluctant to give his account of his journey's events. Finally, however, he realized that he could not do otherwise. He related the meeting with humanity as it truly happened.

When she learned the truth of the situation, the Moon became enraged with the malicious actions of her messenger. So great was her anger, in fact, that she took a hatchet and lowered it swiftly upon the now trembling hare in order to split his head right between the ears. The rage of the Moon, however, blinded her judgement, and the hatchet fell short of its mark. Instead of falling upon the crown of the hare's head, the hatchet met with the hare's upper lip and cut him severely. The hare was stirred to a rage of his own. He raised his claws and scratched the Moon's face. The dark spots upon the Moon are the scars from her battle with the hare.

The hare has since made peace with his mistress, for you still can see his outline when you look at the Moon. The hare has always felt, however, that fault lay with humans. A grudge against humanity has been carried in the heart of the hare. In return for the trouble for which he feels humans were responsible, the hare has given the curse of the harelip to the world. It is the hare's way of reminding humans, as he had once tried before, that those who dwell in the holy skies are not ever to be forgotten.

Dyad Moon

The rising of June's lunar cycle is intimately connected with the name of the Moon. Dyad is an archaic word meaning pair.

At this time upon the earth, more than any other, the effects of the Sun and Moon are equally apparent. The Moon that has steadfastly been a symbol of hope still makes her nightly passage across the sky. The effects of the Sun though, are equally apparent with the beginning of the summer months.

In many cultures, the legends of Sun and Moon are also inseparable. Some mythologies consider them to be husband and wife, maid and suitor, or brother and sister. Many consider them interconnected and interdependent.

An Adulterous Moon

BLACKFEET NATIVE AMERICAN TRIBE

The elders tell the tale of the beginnings of all life. The great creator was the Sun. He first created the Moon and took her as his wife. Together, they had seven sons, which can still be seen as the stars of the Big Dipper.

The Creator Sun also gave life to snakes upon the earth. These creatures reproduced so quickly that the lands were soon overrun with their kind. Sun went to the snakes and asked them to slow down. Certainly, the earth could not sustain them if they continued to multiply at such a speedy rate.

The snakes refused to comply with Creator Sun. Failing to gain their cooperation, he decided to destroy them all and free the earth of this burden. And so he did, all but one female snake. This one she-snake was about to give birth and Creator Sun felt compassion for her. She alone was allowed to survive.

One of the snake's descendants, upon reaching adulthood, decided to seek revenge for the destruction of his kind by Creator Sun. To carry out his mission, he assumed a human form. It was in this shape that he came to be known as Snakeman.

In order to avenge his race of ancestors, Snakeman wanted to make Creator Sun suffer a loss as grievous as his own race had suffered in the early times. And so, in his human form, he seduced the Moon.

Sun soon discovered the betrayal and killed Snakeman. Then Sun and his seven sons ran from the Moon. But the Moon had fallen deeply in love with Snakeman. Because Sun had taken the life of her beloved, Moon chased after him with the intention of destroying him as he had destroyed Snakeman.

Sun, who had created Moon and made her powerful, was fearful for the safety of his sons. He armed his sons with powers of their own so that they might defend themselves against the angry Moon. He gave one son a stick that could turn into a forest and another a rock capable of becoming a mountain. He gave his third son a skin filled with water that could turn into a rainstorm, and his fourth son one that could transform into an ocean. His fifth son received a beautiful bird that could change into thunder, lightning, and rain. His sixth son received a pouch of air that could become a mighty windstorm. The last son received a magic power that enabled him to create deep canyons by tracing his finger in the dirt.

As the angry Moon closed her distance on her intended victims, each son used his special power to create an obstacle for her. The Moon overcame each and moved ever closer to her seven sons and their father. When she was almost upon them, one of her sons poured his skin of water and an ocean appeared between them.

Creator Sun took advantage of this distraction to raise himself and his sons into the sky. The Moon, however, was not without powers of her own. She lifted herself into the sky and resumed the chase.

Sun divided the night from the day to gain some rest from the endless pursuit. Through the day, he and his sons can rest from the relentless Moon. At the rise of nightfall she is once again after them, and they seek refuge in the west.

So has it been since the earliest times. We see Sun in his transit across the sky, trying to keep ahead of his angered wife. When the sky turns black, Moon is in pursuit, never failing to track his direction and following nightly the path of his flight. Should this eternal chase ever end, say the elders, it will be a bad omen and would foretell the ending of life itself.

The Parting of Sun and Moon

LITHUANIA

In the beginning of time, before the origin of man, the Sun and Moon were husband and wife. The two lived together along with their daughter, the Earth. They knew nothing but happiness and lived each day fulfilled by their love, each for the other.

As time went by, however, the love that sustained them faded. Sun was displeased with Moon because she was too cold. Moon said that Sun was too hot. Their lives together grew tedious and they drew no satisfaction from each other. The two disenchanted giants agreed to part ways.

There was yet one area in which the estranged lovers shared a common heart. Both Sun and Moon deeply loved their daughter. They argued over who should stay with her when they parted. Each parent so intensely adored the Earth, that they could not come to an agreement as to who should care for the child.

In this time there was a greater god than Sun and Moon, the great god Thunder. Unable to reach a just compromise on their own, they sought Thunder's wisdom. Thunder decided that Sun should care for Earth throughout the day. At nightfall, Moon would watch over their child.

The parting of Sun and Moon has been final. There is not likely to be a reconciliation. However, the judgement of the wise Thunder has endured throughout the ages. Sun and Moon are still bound by his decree.

Mead Moon

The seventh Moon of the year is known as the Mead Moon *and usually rises in July. The Mead Moon rides high at the fullness of the earth's fertility. It is a time when the rewards of the farmer's long hours of labour are most apparent with the ripening of the fields. It is a time of wonder and enchantment, when the miracle of growth and rebirth are evident upon the earth. It is a time of celebration, named for mead, the ancient elixir of the gods. The legends of the Mead Moon are a reflection of this special time of celebration and magic.*

The Tale of Hyuki and Bil

GERMANY

The god Odin set the child of Munddilfore, called Mani, in the sky to drive the chariot of the Moon. Along with the handsome Mani rode two children who he had carried away from the earth when he journeyed skyward. They were the fairest of children: a boy named Hyuki and a girl named Bil.

The children's father, Vidfinner, had sent Hyuki and Bil out into the night to draw the enchanted songmead from Byrger, the magical spring. The two children filled their bucket to the brim with the magic mead. So full was their pail that the treasured mead began to spill over as they lifted their burden on a pole between them.

As Hyuki and Bil descended the mountain spring with their prize, Mani took hold of the children and carried them off to the sky. The wise elders still call out to Bil when the Moon is full. They seek to gain her favour that she might sprinkle a few drops of the magic mead upon their lips so they might gain the wisdom and strength that the magic brew imparts.

Certainly, Hyuki and Bil must still be living upon the face of the Moon. Many believe the dark spots on the Moon are the children's shadows. Many repeat their tale in its original form. Others know it as the nursery rhyme, "Jack and Jill."

The Champion Drinker

Further adventures exist of the song-mead that Hyuki and Bil carried with them to the Moon. They begin with the father of the Moon-children, Vidfinner.

Upon the disappearance of his children, Vidfinner was full of remorse. He grieved, as a father would be expected to grieve. But if the truth be known, it was not his children for whom he lamented, but the song-mead that was lost with them upon the Moon, for Vidfinner was also called Svigdur, the Champion Drinker.

So greatly did he yearn for the magic elixir, that Svigdur put aside his loyalty to the gods. In a rage, he threw himself toward the heavens and attacked the Moon-god without reserve. He was victorious over the god and came away with his prize, the treasured vessel of song-mead. Even the objections of his own son, Hyuki, did not sway Svigdur from his goal. In fact, the child suffered serious injury at the hands of his father.

Svigdur was condemned for his actions and took flight from the revenge of the elder gods. He fled to the fiery land to the South. Having brought the stolen mead with him, Svigdur was most welcome at the Southern gates.

Odin, the chief of the gods, followed Svigdur to the South and through wisdom and stealth recaptured the stolen song-mead. Odin returned the magic mead to its rightful place upon the Moon. As for Svigdur, the gods condemned him. Upon his death, he was denied a place among the honoured dead and decreed to dwell forever upon the face of the Moon.

In his eternal condemnation, Svigdur was reunited with his beloved mead. But the gods have made it as poison to him. He is not the benefactor of the strength and wisdom that the drink might bring to other people, but lives in an eternal state of drunkenness. In this state, he is powerless to defend himself against the eternal beating he endures at the hands of the Moon-god, who he once had slain, but who had been given new life by the elder gods.

Wort Moon

August's lunar cycle is known as the Wort Moon. Wort is an old-world word meaning plant. At the time of this Moon, the earth's fertility is at full maturity and harvest time is at hand.

The legends chosen for the Wort Moon are dedicated to the earth's plant life, and are, most appropriately, tales of the relationship between the Moon and the earth's growing flora and fauna. Through times and cultures, this relationship may change, and the Moon takes on a different role in its relationship to the plant life. Both the Moon and the earth, however, always seem to be interconnected. The plants are necessary for human survival. The Moon, according to some mythologies, has been essential for the survival of plants.

The First Tears

In an age before humans learned to mark time, there lived a lonely orphan child who travelled the earth. He wandered through the lands unloved and alone; no one who crossed his path befriended him. The child's sorrow was great. The pain swelled up inside of him until he thought his small body would burst from its heavy burden.

Today if a child were to carry the weight of this young orphan's loneliness, tears would fall and offer some small release. This young boy, however, could know no relief, for he lived before tears had been created.

As the youth wandered, he was not truly alone. Each night as the Moon ascended his place in the blackened sky, he watched over the young boy. From the depths of his great being, Moon felt pity for the orphan.

One night, Moon did not rise to his nightly station. Instead, he came to the earth to seek out the orphan in his misery. He urged the young boy to let his sorrow flow from him as tears. When the orphan did, the first tears of the world were shed.

"These tears must not fall to the earth," cautioned Moon, "for that is where the people of the fields grow their food. We must not taint the life of the plants with your sorrows, lest your comfort be their demise." Moon caught the tears of the orphan's sorrow on his own massive body. When the acid tears fell to Moon's surface, they left dark stains. If Moon had allowed these tears to touch the earth, the fertile race of plants might never have survived.

When Moon brought the boy release with the first tears, he also bestowed his blessing on the child. From that day on, the child was met with love by all he encountered. For the rest of his life, people cared for him.

As for Moon, the stains of the first tears can still be seen as he rises full. These stains will be as a reminder of the time when Moon protected the plants of the earth with his wisdom.

Moon Waters

Many years ago, there lived a man named Bochica who was highly honoured among the people of the earth. Bochica taught the tribes to build their homes sturdy to protect them from the harsh elements and the night's cold winds. He taught the people to plant their fields with fertile crops and reap the land's bounty at harvest time. In the childhood of humanity, Bochica taught the tribes to care for themselves and no longer turn to the gods for their every need. He turned the human race from helpless children to a proud and productive people.

The great and wise Bochica had a wife named Huythaca, and for many years they lived happily together. A time arrived, however, when their days of love and peace came to an end. No one can be certain what prompted the change, but Huythaca began to feel discontented with her life. Perhaps it was the progression of time, which caused her beauty to wane. Perhaps it was jealousy of her husband's devotion to the people of the soil. Perhaps it was her idleness in the times when Bochica was among the earth's tribes. Whatever the reason, Huythaca became embittered toward her husband and those people to whom he devoted his time and knowledge.

Huythaca caused the waters of the river to overflow the banks. The waters covered the fields that were rich with the crops that would feed the tribes, and flooded the homes that would protect the people from the night air. All of Bochica's work was carried away on the back of the river water. The floods of Huythaca carried off the tribes' good work and washed away many lives.

When Bochica saw the devastation his wife's bitterness had caused, he set out to reverse the waters. He returned the river to its natural state and dried the fertile lands to stay the crops from drowning. The lives of the earth people that the waters had claimed, however, Bochica could not return.

Because of Bochica's love of the earth tribes, the destruction brought upon them by Huythaca deeply wounded him. He grieved for those who were lost as if they were the children of his own blood. But greater than his grief was his anger with Huythaca over the destruction she had caused. Bochica did not let her actions go unpunished.

Bochica turned his wife into the Moon. To add to her dishonour, he gave the earth people the first solar calendar. Those who till the soil now plant their crops in the bright sun and look to the sun to nourish them and make them grow. The Moon can be seen each night making her transit across the sky. When the people look at Huythaca in her place in the heavens, they are reminded of her days of destruction and the importance of the earth's greenery for their survival.

As for Huythaca, her punishment has increased her bitterness. Although Bochica removed her from the lands of the earth people, he could not totally protect them from her wrath. Every now and then, the Moon still causes the waters to swell. The wise tribespeople regard the Moon, as well as the sun, as they plant their fields. Although Huythaca's banishment has diminished her, her power is still among us.

Barley Moon

The Moon of September is the Barley Moon. September is the time of harvesting grains from the fields. When the Barley Moon ascends the blackened sky, people celebrate the fruits of the year's labours.

The legends we dedicate to September's Moon are tales rooted in the harvest. They are the stories of how harvesting came to be a most sacred time in the eyes of the creatures that dwell upon the earth.

Talesin, Birth of a Poet
WALES

Cerridwen, the Moon goddess, prepared a brew of inspiration to give to her son. She culled the proper herbs at the proper time and made all the necessary preparations to complete the magical mixture. It was a long and precise process, and took a year (a lunar year) and a day, to complete.

The magical brew needed to be stirred constantly. The goddess gave this task to a youth named Gwion Bach. He faithfully stirred the brew for the entire time of preparation. At the end of the year's work, when the potion was at its completion, three drops of the brew flew out of the cauldron onto Gwion's fingers.

Instinctively, he thrust the fingers into his mouth to still the burning pain of the hot brew.

But only the first three drops of this magical brew had the qualities of inspiration that Cerridwen sought for her son. When Gwion thrust his scalded hand into his mouth and tasted the potion, he inadvertently robbed the goddess of her entire year's work.

Enraged, Cerridwen chased Gwion Bach to seek her revenge. With his newly gained wisdom from the magical brew, Gwion hid from the Moon goddess by taking the forms of various animals. The goddess, close in pursuit, did some shape changing of her own. At last Gwion, in the form of a bird, saw a grain pile on a barn floor. Just as Cerridwen, in her form as a hawk, was about to capture Gwion, he dove toward the grain pile.

Some say that it was corn that lay upon the barn floor. Some recall it as wheat, and yet others tell the story of a pile of barley. In any case, Gwion Bach became a grain and hid himself amid the pile. Cerridwen followed Gwion to the grain pile and changed herself into a black hen. In this form, she discovered Gwion and swallowed him up.

Nine months later, the Moon goddess gave birth to Gwion as Talesin. Her anger with Gwion had not faded and, upon his rebirth, it was her intention to seek her revenge once more. When the child emerged, however, Cerridwen could not bear to harm him. She was so taken by his beauty that she spared him the wrath of her anger. Talesin went on to become one of the first and certainly one of the most accomplished of the Welsh bards.

Each year when the Barley Moon rises in September, we are reminded of the death of the grain at harvest time, much as we remember the demise of Gwion Bach at the hands of the Moon goddess. Nine months later, the earth is in midsummer, at the height of fertility, as reflected in the birth of the poet, Talesin. Each year the Moon goddess consumes Gwion Bach and the barley is gone from the fields. Each year, Talesin is reborn and so is the earth made fertile once again.

The Barley Mother

ANCIENT GREECE

Demeter, a lunar goddess, has ancient ties to barley. Her name is derived from the word deai, which means barley.

The story is told of when Demeter created the first seasons upon the earth. Each year reflects the death of the plants in the fields with the coming of winter and their rebirth in spring—but it was not always as we know it. At one time, no seasons existed; the earth was rich and fertile throughout the year. It was always warm and pleasant and all the world was vibrant with life. This was the work of Demeter, for the goddess loved the earth and watched over it tenderly.

Persephone, Demeter's daughter, also loved the earth. She spent hours playing in Demeter's fertile flower fields. If there was anything that enriched Demeter's heart more than her beloved earth, it was her love for her beautiful daughter.

The Barley Mother was not alone in her love of Persephone. Hades, god of the underworld, was also taken by the maiden's great beauty. As he watched her from his underworld kingdom, the dark god became more and more obsessed with her beauty. He made plans to carry her away to the underworld to spend all of eternity with him.

One day, as Persephone was playing amid her beloved flowers, the earth opened up. From out of the crevice arose Hades in his great chariot drawn by black horses. He swept up the maiden in his strong arms and turned his black stallions back toward the underworld. Having collected his prize and headed safely back toward his own kingdom, the earth closed up behind him so none could follow.

Upon learning of the loss of her daughter, Demeter was consumed by grief. In her great sadness, the goddess neglected her beloved earth. The fertile lands grew barren. The warm air grew cold. The vibrancy of life began to give way to the icy hand of death.

Zeus, the father of all the gods, saw the great sadness of the goddess and her neglect of the earth that she so dearly loved. He knew that this was not good and should not be allowed to continue. Zeus sent his messengers to the underworld kingdom to persuade Hades to release Persephone back to the care of her mother. At first, the god of the underworld refused. Finally, however, he consented to yield to the father god's wishes.

Before releasing Persephone back into the bright world of her mother, however, Hades gave her a taste of a magic pomegranate. Through the magic of the fruit, Persephone became destined to spend part of every year in the kingdom of the dark god.

Upon the return of her daughter, Demeter was gladdened. She stopped neglecting the lands of the earth and fertility was returned to the fields. But the curse of the magic pomegranate continues. Each year, Persephone must return to Hades' underworld kingdom. When she does, Demeter grieves. She neglects the earth's green lands and they fall barren in winter.

When Perephone's time in the underworld is done, she returns to her mother. The birds are the first to hear the footsteps of the maiden as she makes her way back from the underworld. That is why they herald the spring with their singing. When Persephone returns, Demeter's time of grief ends and the Barley Mother again tends to her beloved earth. So has it been each year, and so shall it continue. Unless the curse of the pomegranate is broken, the autumn months will announce the beginning of the earth's barrenness, and spring will continue to ease Demeter's pain and herald the rebirth of fertility upon her earth.

Blood Moon

The lunar cycle of October is that of the Blood Moon; its legends are of death. During the Blood Moon, the changes of the earth make visible the first signs of winter's arrival. The trees' changing colours and the air's crispness herald the winter season. All that live upon the earth make ready for winter's time of dominion. The squirrels hurriedly gather any last bits of food before the snows hide it away from their reach. Those who slumber through the cold months have made ready their beds. The birds have already taken to the air in search of the warmer lands to the south. People have taken their grain to the winter store and sealed their dwelling tightly against the bitter, biting chill of the winter winds. The earth has begun to fall to barrenness, and people will turn to the hunt for their sustenance. In this time, when all the world works feverishly to prepare for the coming season, the elders dedicate their tales to the Blood Moon.

A Lesson of Darkness

INUITS OF THE BERING STRAIT

Tulugaukuk, the Raven Father, was the creator of all life. Raven visualised the world covered with growing plants. He created trees, vines, and bushes to beautify the lands of the earth. From out of one of the pea pods, Man was born. When Raven saw this creature, he cared for him.

Raven showed Man the worlds of his creation, including a Sky-Land. In it, there was a round hole. Around the hole was short grass that glowed like white flame. On one edge of the hole, some grass was missing. Raven explained to Man that this was the star called Moon. Raven had taken some of the fire-grass to the land below to create the first fire on the earth.

Raven Father fed Man with salmon berries and heath berries, which he had made plentiful in the forests. Man tasted the berries and his hunger was satisfied. There was fresh water in the clear lakes for Man to drink.

Next, Raven collected clay and shaped two mountain sheep with his hands. Raven called on Man to look at his new creation. Man was pleased at this new form of life. Raven wondered if people would kill the sheep if they became plentiful. He thought they might, so he sent the sheep to live among the steep rocks where few people could reach them.

With more clay, Raven formed reindeer, caribou, muskrat, and all the other beasts of the land, water, and air. In time, Raven became afraid that Man would kill the creatures of his making and use them for food and clothing. He took white clay and shaped it into a bear, the guardian spirit of the animals. Raven warned Man not to disturb White Bear, for he would tear Man to pieces with his sharp claws.

The numbers of the earth people grew steadily. Soon many people lived upon the earth. As Raven feared, they began killing the animals of his creation. As punishment, Raven took the light away from the Sky-Land and plunged the earth into darkness. The people of earth made offerings to Raven so that he would return the light to the earth, but he would not.

Finally, the son of Raven took pity on the earth people. The Raven Boy took the leather bag in which the

Creator had hidden the Sun and flew far into the sky. When he reached the place where the sun should be, he tore open the leather bag and the light burst forth. Raven Father called after the boy. Thinking that his son had stolen the sun for himself, Raven told him not to allow it always to be dark.

Perhaps out of a misunderstanding or perhaps to honour his father whose wishes he had first stood against, Raven Boy toppled the sky. Sometimes the Sun is visible through the spinning Sky-Land, sometimes it is the Moon, the round hole with white fire that less brightly lights the earth. It is sometimes dark and sometimes bright. But as Raven Father wished, there is not always darkness upon the earth.

People still hunt. The Sun and Moon still take their turns being visible above. But we hope the lessons of the Raven Father have been learned well. We hope that people hunt the creatures of the Creator no more than is dictated by their needs. We hope they honour the White Bear and remember the lesson of darkness.

The Blood of Creation

When the earth was first formed, it was covered with darkness. There was no light, only earth and sky. The earth and sky lay close together, as a husband and wife whose love makes them as one. People were very small and lived squeezed tightly between the two great lovers. As people moved upon the earth, they bumped their heads on the sky's clouds.

At last, the people grew tired of living in such tight spaces. One of them, called Lingo, took it upon himself to remedy the situation. With his brothers' help, he raised the clouds higher above the earth so that people

could walk upright without the sky forever knocking against them. Having been successful with the resolution to the first problem, Lingo decided to tackle the problem of eternal darkness as well.

Lingo thought about what he could use to make lanterns to hang in the sky. When he came upon the great tree called Huppe Piyer, he had his answer. In time, with the aid of his twelve brothers and the thirteen Bhimul brothers, the great tree was felled. The men cut two great circles from the tree and stripped off the bark. The circles were prepared to turn into great lights for the sky.

The brothers wanted to animate the lanterns so that they might move unaided across the sky. After discussing it thoroughly, they came to the realization that it would take life to instill life. They decided to take the newborn son of a villager named Mahapurab to complete their work.

Lingo stole the child from Mahapurab, brought him to the place where the lantern-discs lay in readiness, and killed him. He offered the blood of the child to the two discs to drink. The larger disc, which was male, drank freely of the child's blood. The smaller disc, a woman, drank only a little. The big appetite of one circle was to become the Sun; the blood it drank is responsible for its bright red colour. The Moon, who drank only a little of the blood offering, is always pale.

As for Mahapurab and his wife, they grieved but for a short time. They looked up in the sky at the bright Sun and recognized their child. They never again knew sorrow for their son. They saw him each day and each night transcend the sky and knew that he alone shall know immortality as he lives forever in the Sun and Moon.

Snow Moon

The eleventh lunar cycle is known as the Snow Moon. At this time of the year in Western cultures throughout Europe and North America, the earth is blanketed with the first snows of the winter season. The cold grasp of winter's ice and snow has begun to take hold. It is a difficult time for those who depend upon the kindness of nature for their survival.

Yet in this time the peoples of many cultures do not dwell on the harshness of the season. When they regard the white Moon in the heavens, they may not see a reflection of the ice and snow that makes each day a challenge to their continued survival. They may see, instead, the silver light of hope. They look upon the Snow Moon and know in their hearts that the winter will not last forever; the warmth of spring will once again rule the lands.

The legends of the Snow Moon are stories of transition and hope. The tales reflect an ending to the frozen grip of winter and herald the beginning of hope and warmth and, perhaps, love.

St. Dwnywen's Ice

Many believe that St. Dwnywen is a canonized version of an earlier Moon goddess of the Welsh people.

Dwnywen was deeply in love with a Welsh prince, and he returned her love without reserve. Were it left to the hearts of these young lovers, they would be as one and never be parted one from the other. But in these times, it was not the right of a maiden to offer her own heart. It could not be released, according to the ways of the

land, without the blessing of her father. Dwnywen's father would not be convinced that their union was a worthy one, and so it was never to be. Dwnywen's father withheld his consent to their marriage.

The young prince became bitter in his disappointment. Frustrated with the knowledge that he was powerless to change the father's decision, he turned his bitterness toward Dwnywen. This confused and upset Dwnywen to such an extent that she ran away. She fled to the quiet solitude of the forest and lived the life of a hermit.

One day as she slumbered in her forest retreat, Dwnywen had a dream. An angel appeared to her and offered her a magic potion that would fulfill her every desire. In the vision, the angel also offered this potion to Dwnywen's lover, but when he tasted of the elixir, he turned into ice.

The angel then granted Dwnywen three wishes. Her first was that her beloved prince be turned back from ice into human form. Only the truest, deepest love could have inspired such a wish. For her other wishes, Dwnywen turned her thoughts to the lovers of the world. Her second wish was that all lovers be fulfilled in the arms of their beloved or be freed from the spell of love. Her third wish was that lovers should never want to marry. In this time, when a woman's heart was not her own to give, Dwnywen knew too well that her desire for marriage had brought her nothing but pain.

Dwnywen's legend mirrors the time of the Snow Moon upon the earth. Her beloved is turned from ice as the earth is about to be released from the hand of winter. Her wishes for the happiness for lovers is as the hope that the Snow Moon heralds for the coming warmth of spring.

Her tale is one of transition, of change. In the old druid lands stands the church of Llandwwynwen in Anglesey. Here, the festival of St. Dwnywen is celebrated in the dead of winter. In South Wales, her feast is held at the beginning of spring. She is, indeed, a symbol of hope to the Welsh people who remember her story.

The Snow Queen

DENMARK

Some legends remember the Moon as the watchful light that soars above all. She is the hope of the days to come. She is the watchful eye that is ever mindful of the fate of children. She is the bright tomorrow that brings promise through the night sky when the snows fall in winter.

The following tale is similar to many of the ancients' tales, but has been empowered with a special child-like magic such as only could have been derived from the visionary genius of Hans Christian Andersen, the great teller of tales.

In the center of a small village after the fall of a fresh snow, all the children gathered to enjoy sliding and playing on the newly fallen snow. The boldest children attached themselves to the carts of the people who passed; the carts would move along with the children sliding merrily behind.

A boy named Kay noticed a large sled approaching the scene of the winter merriment. The driver was covered from crown to feet in white fur. After circling twice around the laughing children, the driver steered the big sled close enough so that Kay grabbed on and was carried through the snow.

The sled went faster and faster, away from Kay's companions, and right out of the village. The snow began to fall anew. It fell so fast and thick that Kay could not see right in front of him. He tried to let loose of the big sled but somehow he was held fast. He tried to call out for help but no one heard. The snow kept falling and the sled kept moving faster and faster.

Sometimes the big sled jumped and Kay found himself flying through the air over crevices and above the hedges that rose above the snow. Still the sled continued on, never slowing.

Finally, the big sled came to a stop. The driver arose and Kay could see the tall, thin figure of a woman. It was not until then that Kay saw that her adornments of white fur were made of the purest snow. This was the Snow Queen that Kay remembered from the tales his grandfather told to him.

Kay looked all around the strange and magical place the Snow Queen had carried him. Beneath him, he heard the songs of the wind. The wolves howled and the snow sparkled. Above him in the winter sky, the heavens were filled with screaming black crows. Higher still, above the darkness, Kay could see the bright Moon watching over him.

Each day, Kay slept at the feet of the Snow Queen in the land of winter snow. By night, he gazed at the bright Moon above him. So it continued through time. His days were spent in frozen slumber. His nights were filled with the light of hope.

In time Gerda, Kay's closest friend, braved strange lands and unknown perils to rescue him. Until then, the Moon watched over Kay each night to ensure his survival and stay him from losing all hope amid his icy existence.

Children still look to the Moon to watch over them through the night. As Kay was sustained through the endless winter of the Snow Queen, so are children still comforted by the Moon's light through the darkness.

Oak Moon

$\mathcal{T}$he calendar's twelfth lunar cycle ascends to its heavenly station in December. The elders call this time the Oak Moon.

The oak is a symbol of strength and eternity. When the winter is in full reign over the earth, it is important to remember the oak's endurance. To survive the trials of winter, people must find within themselves the oak's great strength.

More than any other religious group, the Druids are remembered for their sacred oak rites. Usually, the Druids are thought to follow a solar deity. Yet in looking at the rites connected with the gathering of the sacred mistletoe from the oak trees, it becomes obvious that their rites were not performed without the blessing of the Moon. The proper time for the collection of mistletoe was on the sixth day of the full Moon. The mistletoe could only be cut with a golden sickle. Although gold is considered a metal sacred to the Sun, the golden ritual tool used was in the shape of the Moon's crescent.

The legends of the Oak Moon are the stories of the tree from which December's Moon derives its name. They are the tales of the mighty oak.

A Tale of the Oak Spirit

PRE-CHRISTIAN GREAT BRITAIN

Three young boys went into the woods when the Moon was high. They were filled with the energy of youth and began breaking slender saplings as they ran through the trees. Their rambunctious romp continued until one of the youths came upon an old horn lying on the ground. The instrument was of an old style, made from the horn of an animal.

Over the fearful objections of his companions, the boy decided to try it out. He put his lips to the ancient instrument and blew. The sound that issued from the horn was an eerie, unearthly groan. The sound by itself was enough to make the three friends turn and flee, but when the horn was sounded, there came a far better reason to take flight.

In response to the horn's call, a terrible shout from deep in the wood rang out and the sound of hunting hounds in pursuit of their prey could be heard. Two of the boys instinctively ran as fast as they could toward the forest edge. The one who had sounded the hellish instrument stood frozen with fear for a moment before he regained his senses and took off after his companions. Behind him, he could hear footsteps closing quickly. Frightened and stumbling, his legs never stopped moving as he raced from the dark figure that now followed him.

In the meantime, the two boys who were ahead emerged safely from the wood. They ran to the first dwelling they could find: a church that sat just outside the forest. There they tightly shut the big door and waited for their friend.

Huddled behind the heavy door, the boys could hear their friend nearing, and they could hear his pursuer close behind. Just a few steps from the door, they heard the Hunter stop. They heard the swish of an arrow as it cut through the night air. Quickly, they opened the door. They saw their friend lying face down on the steps, dead. There was no arrow. There was no wound. There were no hounds. There was no Hunter—just the full Moon shining brightly over her beloved woods.

The antlered shadow of Herne the Hunter can still be seen in the forest when the Moon is full. Perhaps it is the light of Diana, the ancient Roman lunar goddess, that gives life to the oak spirit. In any case, it is possible to see the dark silhouette of the Hunter among the oak branches by moonlight—even if you would prefer not to encounter his shadowy figure.

Mistletoe, the Fruit of the Oak

GERMANY

Many cultures highly valued the mistletoe. Part of its magic was that it grew neither in the earth nor in the heavens, but was perched upon the oak between earth and sky. Some thought the mistletoe contained the life spirit of the oak, for in the winter months, when the oak was void of leaves, the mistletoe was still green. German mythology recalls the mistletoe's part in the drama of Frigga, the lunar goddess, and Baldur, her son.

Frigga was very protective of her son. A fair part of her concern was rooted in a vision she had had of her son's death. Although the goddess was gifted with foresight of the future, she was unable to change the visions she saw.

In an attempt to remove the possibility of losing her son, Frigga began to extract a promise from all the creatures of the world that they would never harm Baldur. She sent her maids to extract a vow from the living creatures, plants, and even from metals. All things promised to spare the life of Baldur, save the mistletoe. From the mistletoe, no promise was requested. This was a slender creature, so weak that it had to cling to the side of a strong oak tree for protection. From such a delicate being, there was no threat to Baldur. So Frigga was comforted. She had no reason to be concerned for her son's safety.

With no harm that could befall him, Baldur entertained gods and men alike as a target for their sharp spears. Stones and arrows were let fly toward him. When he emerged from behind their flurry, he was unharmed. No stone bruised him. Neither spear nor arrow could pierce his fair skin. All men loved Baldur and each missile that was sailed in his direction was a token of honour. There were few that restrained themselves from the sport of honouring the son of Frigga.

Hodur was one of the few who did not join in the celebration of the fair Baldur. Although he honored the god, Hodur was blind and could not aim his bow in the direction of the bright Baldur. Hodur never took part in the festivities, until one day at Loki's encouragement.

Now, Loki was an evil god—a god who delighted in chaos and destruction. Unbeknown to the blind Hodur, Loki had fashioned an arrow out of mistletoe, the only creature from which no vow of protection had been extracted. Loki placed the arrow in Hodur's bow, and held the blind archer's arm so that his aim was true. When the special arrow struck the beautiful Baldur, he fell to the slumber of death.

Frigga was sorrowful but could do nothing to bring her son back from Hela, the land of the dead. The mistletoe still survives as a reminder of the tale of the beautiful Baldur, the bright son of the Moon goddess.

Wine Moon

*B*ecause the lunar calendar does not coincide with the solar year, there are often thirteen Moons in the year. The common expression "once in a blue moon" refers to this extra Moon, which occurs only once in every two-and-a-half years. Most often, when the thirteenth Moon occurs, it is in the longer months of thirty-one days. The thirteenth Moon never rises in the short month of February and seldom in the shorter months of April, June, September, and November.

Although Blue Moon might be a term easily recognized, some know the thirteenth Moon as the Wine Moon. The original explanation given through oral tradition of this name is rooted in the supposed origin of wine. Some say that wine was the first gift of luxury the gods gave to humans. When there is an extra Moon in the year, it is a gift of time. Time is, perhaps, the greatest luxury of all. It is, therefore, fitting that we know the thirteenth Moon as the Wine Moon.

The Wine of Indra

INDIA

Through many cultures, many gods truly adored the fruit of the vine. Few thirsted for it as deeply as the Indian god Indra; he would drink thirty bowls of wine before going into battle against demons.

A magical quality existed in the sweet nectar. According to the oldest Indian legends, wine had the power to make the gods immortal. Even its consumption was magical. Originally, it was drunk from a bowl that constantly refilled itself. This bowl eventually became four cups in honour of the four phases of the Moon.

Fortified by the magic elixir, Indra rode his golden chariot to the lands of India. There he found Vritra, the drought-demon, holding the land's seven great rivers prisoner. Indra slew the drought-demon in battle and released the rivers to flow once more. He also freed the sacred cattle that were the rain clouds, and he slew Vala, the demon who had stolen the rain clouds from the sky and hidden them in the mountain of Vritra.

When the waters of the earth were free to flow once again in the riverbeds and from the skies, Indra sought out all the other *asuras*, or demons. The great Indra valiantly fought the evil ones. What the elders say of the wine must certainly be true, for the brave Indra survived his battles and went on to rule over the lands with his beloved wife, Indrani, the Queen of Heaven.

Even today, the effects of the wine must linger. The magical drink still bestows the gift of immortality upon humans. Certainly, there is no more valiant or confident a warrior to be found than the person who is well into his cups.

Destruction and Delight

ANCIENT GREECE

In Greece, Dionysus is known as the god of wine. His gift of the grape grants freedom from that which is rigid. It grants fluidity to the imagination and freedom to the heart. Yet this is a double-edged delight, for there is a tale of the wine god that speaks more of destruction than of ecstasy.

There was a time when pirates came upon the young god Dionysos. Driven by a wickedness, they captured the divine youth. They thought he was the son of one of Zeus' favourite kings. They took Dionysos back to their ship and sought to tie him up. To their surprise, their ropes wouldn't hold the young lord. They fell off his arms and legs, and he stood there, smiling at the pirates with his dark eyes.

When the helmsman saw the ropes drop from Dionysus, he was frightened. He shouted out that this must be a powerful god. He feared that the dark-eyed youth would bring great storms against their ship. Yet, there was no storm. Instead, the most incredible things began to take shape.

First, a river of wine appeared that seemed to flow everywhere about the ship. It was sweet and fragrant and its scent spoke of a personage divine. Then vines sprang up on either side of the vessel, all the way to the

top of the mast. Ripe grapes covered the vines and garlands of flowers covered the oars. The crew became frightened and realized there was no way that they could pilot their ship. They screamed for the helmsman to steer them to shore and to the safety of dry land.

It was then that Dionysus became a lion. He seized the captain in his great teeth. The rest of the crew jumped in the sea to escape the wrath of the wine god. When they did, they became dolphins. Only the helmsman was spared.

And so it is with the gift of Dionysus. Although it is a gift of luxury, it is also a gift of idleness. The delight of luxury may at any time give way to the destruction of decadence.

PART 2:
Lunar
Dignitaries

Divine Personages

Among the African Bushmen, the creator god was a praying mantis god called !kaggen. At night, he walked beneath the desert sky. To help out the world and humanity, one night !kaggen took off his shoe and flung it into the sky. By doing this, he created the Moon, which became known as !kaggen's shoe. The Moon's waxing and waning are recognized as the sign of !kaggen's footprint walking across the heavens. What better symbol to record the movement of the Moon than the footprint of a god?

Other cultures throughout history have also seen the mark of a divine personage in the Moon. To some, the Moon is a symbol of a deity. To others, it is the actual essence of the deity. However different times and cultures perceive the Moon, the Moon's divine character, it seems, always has been with us. Known by many names and in many characters, the lunar dignitaries always have held humankind's heart and dreams.

The legends of the lunar dignitaries are many. Though the faces change through the procession of time, their ability to lure humans with their sorcery has never faded.

Thoth

ANCIENT EGYPT

Many past cultures recognize the spirit of the Moon as a goddess. Examples can be seen in Diana, the ancient Roman Moon goddess, and in Artemis, a lunar deity of Ancient Greece.

This is not true, however, of all of the ancient civilizations. Thoth, the Egyptian god, is well known as the patron of science, literature, and invention and the keeper of the ancient wisdom. He is often recognized as the keeper of records and the scribe, messenger, and spokesman of the Egyptian gods. However, in one of his aspects Thoth is also a Moon god.

The following tale relates the origins of Thoth, the Moon god.

In the earliest times, Re, the sun god, lived happily upon the earth among humans. As he grew old, people began to regard him as weak. They plotted to raise their hands against him and questioned his divine authority. After asking the goddess Hathor to teach the mortal subjects of his kingdom a lesson, Re found that he was still filled with discontent toward the people of the earth. Re took his problem to Nun, the watery abyss. Nun bid Nut, his daughter and goddess of the sky, to assume the shape of a cow and bear Re on her back.

Upon Re's retreat from the earth, a few people took up their weapons against Re's enemies. When the god saw what was happening on the earth, he declared the beginning of the slaughter. It has, from that day, continued among humans.

Meanwhile, from his place upon the back of Nut, Re created the heavenly bodies and positioned himself in a place to observe the people of earth. All went well at first. But in time, Nut was overcome with dizziness at the height. Re created special deities to support Nut in the heavens. He created Shu, the god of the air, and positioned him beneath the divine cow goddess to keep her aloft. Geb was also created to look after the earth.

All was not yet perfect, however. By his withdrawal from the earth, Re had taken his light from its inhabitants. There had to be some arrangements made to fill this need in his absence.

Re sent for the god Thoth. He told Thoth that while he was in the netherworld, the needs of the earth must still be watched over. To fulfill this purpose, Thoth was sent to the earth as Re's divine agent. It was Thoth's responsibility to oversee all who dwelt upon the earth and handle any trouble that arose. He was also required to provide the earth with light in Re's absence. For this reason, the Moon of Thoth came into being.

To this day, the eye of Re can be seen by day as the sun that shines above the earth. When Re retreats to the netherworld, it is the Moon that sheds its light as the god Thoth watches over the earth.

Brigit, the Enchantress
Celtic Ireland

Brigit, Bride, Brede, Bridget, Brizo—history has known this goddess by many different names and has credited dozens of different attributes to her divine figure.

Medieval Irish poets have recognized her as the Triple Muse and looked to her as their patron. Her three aspects were the goddess of poetry, the goddess of healing, and the goddess of the blacksmith's craft. In Scotland, she could be recognized as the Mother Goddess. She was the Bride of the Golden Hair or the Bride of the White Hills and was known by her symbol of purity, the white swan.

Other cultures have recognized Brigit as a sea goddess, the goddess of small animals, and the patron of childbirth. She seems to be descended, however, from the goddess Brizo of Delos. This may be where she gets her present associations to the Moon and sea. Brizo was a lunar deity to whom ships were given in offering. Her name was derived from the Greek word *brizein*, which means to enchant.

Throughout history, the Moon and sea evoke feelings of mystery and magic. This is, in part, due to the incredible visions painted by poets and artists throughout time. One of the most widely known examples is "Die Lorelei" by Heinrich Heine. The poet writes of the unparalleled beauty of a maiden of the sea, a mermaid. His imagery embodies all the enchantments of the ages and the wonder and magic of the waters in the melodic voice and the mysteriously captivating countenance of this strange and beautiful creature of the watery realms.

The long association with enchantment and mystery may be one factor in the survival of Brigit through the centuries. Even at the time when the new era of Christian theology was uprooting the old ways of worship, those who followed the religion of the land would not betray their goddess. The only way the new ways of Christianity could take hold among the common people was to incorporate the goddess into their own doctrine. Brigit then became known as Saint Bridget.

Even after her canonization, however, the goddess retained her previous virtues. A Cornish invocation against scalds and burns asks the aid of the triple goddess Brigit. Today many still use this charm.

Though the names by which humanity might know the goddess are ever changing, the goddess herself has always endured. Those who practice the blacksmith's trade still remember that if ever the glowing iron is turned against them or the sparks fly from the furnace and sear their flesh, they need only repeat those words that they learned in their childhood and their patron, Brigit, will heed their call.

> *Three Ladies came from the east,*
> *One with fire, and two with frost.*
> *Out with the fire, and in with thee frost.*

# Diana

ANCIENT ROME

Diana is the Moon goddess of the ancient Romans. The root word of her name is *di*, which means bright. It is a title most befitting a goddess of the Moon.

Diana's name has survived through the rise and fall of several civilizations and has filtered down through time in several different forms. In *Aradia: Gospel of the Witches,* by Charles Leland (Bantam Books, 1971), Diana is called Tana. In the writings of Shakespeare, she survives as Titania, the Queen of the Faeries.

In much of the religious art of the Roman era, Diana is depicted with a stag beside her. She was a

Goddess of the Wood and Goddess of all the Horned Beasts. Those animals especially sacred to her are those that have horns, for their horns are reminiscent of the sickle Moon that is her symbol.

By her association with the woodland creatures, Diana became the Huntress goddess. She is the patroness of creatures that make their home in the shelter of the forest, and is, therefore, the goddess to whom the hunters must make offering for a successful hunt—she is the patroness of the hunters as well as the hunted.

As in other cultures, the Romans, in their worship of the Moon goddess, saw a connection between the Moon and Sun. This can readily be seen in the tale of Aradia, Diana's daughter, and the first of the witches upon the earth:

> *Diana was a sister to Lucifer, the Lord of Light. She loved her brother from the depth of her being, and she lay down with him. In the turning of the wheel of time, she bore him a fine daughter and called her Aradia. With the inherited light of wisdom from her father—the sun—and her mother—the Moon—Aradia became a mortal and taught her parents' ways upon the earth.*

The arcane mysteries, in light of this legend, may be considered a gift given through the divine love of the Moon goddess, Diana.

Lucifer, as the brother and consort of Diana, is most certainly the product of a world in transition. The above legend must have been borne out of a time of change, a time when the mythology of one time began to give way to another. Legends, cultures, and even different worlds of religious thought overlap.

In *The Golden Bough* (Macmillan, 1922), author Sir James Frazer indicates that Virbius was the true Roman consort of the Woodland goddess (time has preserved little more than his name). Some of the legends that have not faded through the centuries show Pan, the Greek god, as Diana's lover. Other tales depict her in the arms of Apollo, the Greek god of the Sun. These surviving legends are not the original mythology, for Diana is a daughter of Rome, while her supposed consorts come from Grecian mythology.

These legends may, however, be an indication of how deeply Diana's people loved her. They may be symbolic of the marriage between Greek and Roman cultures. In Delos, Greece, remnants exist of great temples erected for the worship of Diana. This is of notable significance because Delos is the homeland of Artemis, the Greek Moon goddess and Diana's counterpart. The Roman goddess was not of equal stature to the Greek Artemis in her own domain; to give a foreign goddess a temple within the kingdom of a native deity's realm was a great honour.

Through her development, Diana is seen to take on many different attributes. In the beginning, she was viewed as the Maiden goddess, protector of chastity. As her role as the patron of animals led to her new position as the Huntress goddess, so did the defender of chastity become the patroness of women in childbirth. As such, she was the goddess of both innocence and fertility.

As many of the other Moon goddesses, a high regard exists for Diana as an enchantress, the Queen of Magic. Leland's *Aradia: Gospel of the Witches* includes a number of incantations to recite to Diana to gain her favour in magical rites.

Sometimes within a single culture, several Moon goddesses were worshipped side by side; they were viewed as aspects of one another. As the Moon changes phases, so does the goddess adopt a new form and a new name according to the needs of her people. In Roman legend, these faces are called *Diana* for the full moon, *Luna* for the crescent phase, and *Herodias* when the moon is dark.

Diana established herself in a position of prominence even outside her Roman countryside. In England, a legend exists that traces the royal Britons back to the Trojans. At the time of the fall of Troy, Prince Brutus—at the direction of the goddess Diana— sought refuge in the area we now know as London. The London Stone, which is preserved today, is believed to be the altar that Prince Brutus erected to Diana in gratitude for guiding him safely to the land that was to become his kingdom.

In all lunar lore, and in the customs carried through today in praise of Diana, the goddess still sits upon her divine throne. Through the love and honour apparent yet today, the mysterious light that sheds its silver glow upon the darkened earth has never faded. In some ways, the symbol of the huntress, Diana, may far outshine the sun.

Artemis, the Divine Archer

ANCIENT GREECE

The legend of Artemis, the Moon goddess of ancient Greece, begins with the amourous adventures of Zeus, the father of all the Olympian kingdom.

Zeus had a passion for the charms of women with beauty and grace. On the earth below the great kingdom of Olympus lived Leto, the fairest of all who dwelt among gods and men. Zeus looked upon her radiance and knew that he must have this mortal. He descended from his kingdom and laid down with the lovely maid.

In time, Leto found that she was to bear Zeus' offspring. The mighty god was pleased at the passing of this blessing. At the same time, however, he feared for the lovely Leto. When Hera, the wife of the mighty god, learned of his infidelity to her, she would certainly turn her wrath upon the radiant mortal.

No one would give Leto sanctuary for fear of angering Hera toward themselves as well. Finally, when the time of the birth was almost at hand, a tiny island agreed to accept the woman in her time of need. In order to express his gratitude, Zeus gave anchor to the island by causing four great pillars to rise up from the sea. Here it was that Leto gave birth to the twin gods Apollo, the Sun God, and Artemis, the Moon goddess.

Throughout their youth, the twins of light were inseparable. Together, they learned the ways of the forest. Artemis learned a great many things from her beloved brother. She learned to use the bow and, in time, far exceeded him with her archery skills. She is still known throughout the world as the Queen of the Bow.

○ ○ ○

As the ways of humans change, so change the needs that they look to their gods to fulfill. Artemis adopted many aspects so she might care for the needs of all.

The Artemis of the Ephesians wore a necklace of acorns that symbolized her association with the forest lands. In this aspect, she was the fair and chaste huntress. She was, however, also seen in another of her aspects as many-breasted, a goddess of fertility and patroness of childbirth.

In Sparta, the goddess was worshipped as Artemis Orithia. In this aspect, she was a Moon goddess. The legend says two Spartan princes found her image carved in a wooden statue in a thicket of willows. (The willow is traditionally held as sacred to the Moon). The young princes were so taken by fear at seeing her image that they were driven mad. Once every year, the young men of the Spartan lands gathered before this wooden likeness of the goddess in remembrance of the two princes. They underwent ritual scourging to drive away the evil that caused madness in the presence of a goddess of purity.

The Taurian Artemis was a dark goddess who demanded human sacrifice. If no sacrifice were offered, she was certain to turn her wrath toward the people of the earth. In time, however, ritual scourging replaced sacrifice as an acceptable token to the goddess.

The actual meaning of the name Artemis is somewhat obscure. Some researchers trace its translation to "source of water." This is congruent with the ancient belief that the Moon is ruler of the tides and all the earth's waters.

Engraved on the statue of Artemis at her Ephesian temple were characters that have come to be known as the Ephesian Letters. Their translation has been lost with time. Many believe, however, that these letters were of great magical significance and that magicians used them in the art of banishment.

The Mother of Fertility, Patroness of Childbirth, Moon Goddess, Huntress, and Mistress of Enchantment and Sorcery still survive, embodied in the form of Artemis, the Divine Archer, Queen of the Bow.

Shing-Moo
ANCIENT CHINA

The legends of the Western world's Moon goddesses are well known and widely published. Untold numbers of writings have preserved the names of these divine beings, and students peruse their mythology. The Far East has a Moon goddess as well. Although the occidental student of mythology seldom hears her name, in China she is called Shing-Moo.

Shing-Moo is the most widely known and revered goddess of the ancient Chinese people. She is known to her followers as the Holy Mother Goddess or as the Perfect Intelligence.

Like some of the other Moon goddesses, the appearance of Shing-Moo bears a remarkable resemblance to the generally accepted image of the Christ child's mother (although Shing-Moo far pre-dates Christianity). Shing-Moo is usually depicted as a veiled figure with the glow of divine serenity about her head. She carries a child in her hands or sometimes on her lap.

The story of Shing-Moo, as well as her appearance, is reminiscent of the Blessed Virgin Mary of the Christian faith. And like the Virgin Mary, Shing-Moo conceived and gave birth to a son while she was still a virgin.

The Christian fathers will, to some extent, acknowledge the Virgin Mary as a Moon goddess. The words of Pope Innocent III make this aspect of the Virgin quite evident: "Toward the moon it is he should look, who is buried in the shadow of sin and iniquity. Having lost divine grace, the day disappears, there is no more sun for him; but the moon is still in the horizon. Let him address himself to Mary; under her influence thousands every day find their way to God."

Shing-Moo has a rightful place beside her sister Moon goddesses of all civilizations rooted in antiquity. Like many other virgin goddesses, she is attributed with the fertility of humans, with love, and with the virtues of maidenhood.

Shing-Moo reflects the same virtues of the Western Virgin. She should, perhaps, be remembered as the Asian ancestor of the West's religions. Because of the virtues she held before the advent of Christianity, Shing-Moo is exceedingly important to Western religious opinion. She and her pre-Christian sister goddesses of many cultures may be thought of as the virgin mothers to the Virgin Mother. They held her virtues for humans before the advent of the Blessed Virgin. In honour of the virtues of Shing-Moo, East not only meets West, but in fact has given birth to it.

Cybele, the Lioness

ANCIENT PHRYGIA

The goddess Cybele was worshipped in Phrygia before 900 B.C. She is known as a goddess of the earth and Moon. The earliest illustrations of this deity show the body of a naked woman and the head of a lion. Later depictions show a woman's form seated upon a throne carved with a lion's face. Still other illustrations depict the goddess in a golden chariot being drawn by lions. The lion embodies the goddess' more primitive nature.

The lion shows her in an aspect of strength and brutality. Cybele can rouse a mortal's heart to terror as well as to love.

This primitive side of the goddess is seen in a study of those who worshipped her. A priesthood of eunuchs was given to her service. On the third day of the festival Dies Sanguinis, ritual dancing and chanting rose to a frenzied pace—to the height of primitive abandon. When the emotional frenzy of the rites reached its peak, the young men who offered these rites to Cybele's honour used knives to inflict wounds upon themselves. Some of the more zealous participants offered the highest sacrifice to their goddess. After castrating themselves, they cast the severed parts at the feet of the goddess' statue. Others ran bleeding into the streets and threw the bloody parts into houses as they passed. These households were bound by tradition to supply the young men with women's clothing. Because of their act of supreme dedication to the goddess, the men were accepted into Cybele's priesthood and wore women's clothing from that day forward.

Often in history, including opposite traits in a deity's rites illustrated the god's or goddess' attributes. In the case of Cybele, the eunuchs who did her honour and made up her priesthood celebrated the goddess' power of fertility. They offered their own fertility to emphasize the goddess' fertile power.

Cybele's fertility aspect becomes even more evident in a study of the words spoken to her honour in her rites of worship. Through his writings, Clement of Alexandria, an early Greek Christian church father and theologian, has preserved the following remnant from Cybele's worship ceremonies:

I have eaten from the timbrel,
I have drunk from the cymbal,
I have borne the sacred vessel,
I have entered into the bridal chamber.

The first two lines refer to a rite that is the predecessor of the Christian sacrament of Holy Communion. The participants partook of a cake made from grain and drank from the fruit of the grape. In one sense, this may have been a rite of thanksgiving to the goddess, because the fertility of the earth was believed to have sprung from her womb.

There is, however, another possible meaning for this ancient rite. The goddess Cybele was known to be the mother of Attis. Some historians believe the wine represents her son's blood and the grain represents his flesh. In such a case, the rite of cake and wine might be considered the direct forerunner of the comparable Christian ceremony. In both ceremonies, the participants partake of the body and blood of a divine son, whether in token or through some magical transformation.

The recitation's third line refers to an ancient ritual bowl, which was sacred to the goddess. The bowl was divided into compartments and was intended to hold various fruits and grains. In the dish's center was a candle set aflame to represent the light of fertility. Again, the goddess' fertility aspect is emphasized. Beneath her radiance, all the fruits of the earth ripen into their fullness.

The oration's final line refers to what is known as the sacred marriage—a total union and devotion with the creative power of the goddess. The priests of Cybele dedicated their most precious asset, their own ability for procreation, to their goddess. The sacrifice among the priests in her service continually renewed Cybele's fertility. In return for their devotion, the goddess bestowed upon them the fertility of spirit.

The fertility of the lion goddess is also clear in her symbol. Many Moon deities are known by their signature of the lunar crescent. In the case of Cybele, the Moon is seen in constant unity with the sun. Since the lunar body is traditionally a female symbol, and the sun is most often male, their union in the representation of Cybele speaks of fertility and the creation of life.

The lioness takes a unique place among the gods and goddesses of mythological history. She is the essence of womankind and femininity but is endowed with the strength and some of the virtues generally associated with male divinities. Where the goddesses of many ancient cultures close their rites to men's eyes, Cybele demands that an all-male priesthood enter into her service.

The impressive figure of the lioness is yet remembered for centuries beyond her own. In many still to come, it is unlikely that her name will become lost or forgotten. Though the people that did her honour are no more, in history and mythology the name of Cybele, the Lioness, endures.

Sinn

ANCIENT BABYLONIA

According to records, for a number of centuries Sinn was the major deity in the Babylonian culture. His worship began about 1800 B.C. and continued well into the thirteenth century B.C.

During his long reign, Sinn enjoyed a position of supremacy over all of Babylonia. A sun god who emerged during the time of Sinn's worship was considered a secondary deity. The Moon was of great importance in this ancient culture and Sinn, as its deity, was considered to be the most powerful of all the gods.

Like Zeus of the Greek pantheon, Sinn was the father of the gods. He was the all-powerful Lord of the

Heavens. In Babylonian legends, however, Sinn's position as the supreme deity was not to endure. He eventually lost his place of supremacy to a Moon goddess—Ishtar, the Star of the Morning and daughter of Sinn.

The beginnings of a lunar triad can be seen in the personage of Sinn. The Moon gods or goddesses of other cultures are often seen in triple aspect, which is evident in the case of this early lunar deity, as well. Sinn's aspects were known by the names Anu, Bel, and Ea. Since Sinn predates most of the known Moon deities of all cultures, he may be considered the Father of Aspects.

The names of Sinn's aspects suggest they may have been forerunners of other culture's deities. Anu may be the forerunner of the Celtic goddess known as Ana, Danu, or Don. The Sinn aspect Bel may be the forerunner of Bile or Beli. Ea may have been the true ancestor of the Germanic tribes' Oestre, whose festival of spring we now know as the Christian festival of Easter. If these suspected lineages are correct, Sinn might be rightly endowed with the title Father of the gods.

Sinn's personality and his relationship to his people change along with his lunar phases. When the Moon rises full, Sinn is a beneficial god. He represents all that is good and is a god of justice, truth, growth, and fertility. When the Moon is dark, however, Sinn brings destruction to the earth. He causes flood, famine, and death.

Even in the dark times, however, Sinn is a god of majesty. His reign extends beyond the lands of the earth. Some say that the earth is deprived of light because Sinn must devote part of his time to giving light to the underworld. He is the judge of the dead and carries those souls worthy of redemption to a land of salvation in the sun. These souls are taken in his Moon boat when he makes his return to the upper world. Even in his darkest aspect, Sinn is a symbol of hope and immortality.

One of the chief necessities in ancient cultures was fertility, which was needed to ensure crop growth and livestock reproduction. Fertility was one of the concerns of the Moon god. In fact, a woman who wished to bear a child often offered her prayers and a gift to Sinn to gain his favour. Without the favour of the Moon god, all the earth might fall.

In some rites, a tribe's female population offered their bodies to the Moon god. This sacrifice would likely be made through a worthy chosen representative such as a king or a priest of Sinn.

On the first night of a marriage, one of Sinn's earthly representatives might take the bride to bed. This was done to ensure the blessing of fertility on the newly united couple.

In time, the reign of Sinn came to an end. In his time of glory, though, the Babylonian people revered him above all else. His ancient hymn still echoes through the lands that once were called Babylon:

Sinn, thou alone givest light from above;
Thou art the light of the world.

$\mathcal{H}$ecate, the $\mathcal{D}$ark One

Hecate is the goddess of night and the Moon in its dark aspect. She is given praise as the Goddess of the Crossroads, the Patroness of Witchcraft and Sorcery, and the Queen of Enchantment.

From the earliest times, Hecate has been associated with occult matters and for this reason her origin is unclear. Many authorities believe her worship began in Thrace, an ancient capital of sorcery in Greece. At any rate, she was highly revered in this area. This reverence, in itself, is a significant factor, for in the overall hierarchy of Mount Olympus, she assumes a relatively minor role. An alternate theory of her origin proposes that she is of pre-Olympic birth. In that case, her place was simply given a lesser position in a newly conceived divine realm.

Unlike many of the other divinities of the past, Hecate, in her dark aspect, has remained relatively free of the adjustments to her personality often deemed necessary by changing cultures. Shakespeare records her in much the same manner as her worshippers over three centuries ago recorded her. Depictions of Hecate often show her in the company of wild dogs, which reflect her connection to the Moon. These dogs are often illustrated as howling, just as dogs are known to bay at the Moon. Her companions are also symbolic of the goddess' dark nature and are almost invariably shown as the darkest black in colour.

Two other symbols belonging to the dark one are the owl and key. The owl reflects the hidden wisdom of all occult matters that the goddess possesses. In fact, to this day, the owl is remembered as a creature of night and of wisdom. The key has been given a dual inter-pretation. It is sometimes thought to be the symbol of the goddess' ability to release or bind the night's phan-tom spirits. It has also been regarded as the key to the door of hidden knowledge.

Because of her ancient ties to the world of occult knowledge, Hecate is still held in high regard as the patroness of those who pursue the ways of witchcraft and magic. Modern occultists often look to the dark goddess for aid in their work, as have many of the ancient practitioners of arcane mysteries.

In the earliest years, after the emergence of Christianity, the Greek poet Ovid wrote about Hecate. In his work, Medea invokes the dark goddess with the following words:

> O night, night, night!
> Whose darkness holds
> All mysteries in shade,
> O flame-lit stars,
> Whose golden rays with Luna floating near
> Are like the fires of day, and you, O Hecate,
> Who know untold desires that work our will
> And art the mistress of our secret spells,
> O Earth who give us bounty of strange grasses,
> Your wandering winds and hills and brooks and wells,
> Gods of the dark-leaved forest and gods of the night,
> Come to my call. When you have entered me,
> As if a miracle had drained their banks and courses,
> I've driven rivers back to springs and fountains.
> I shake the seas or calm them at my will;
> I whip the clouds or make them rise again;
> At my command the winds vanish or return...

Ovid's description of Hecate's great power continues in the finest detail. After reading his verses, it is easy to see why occultists have held so loyally to the service of their patroness. By enlisting the aid of the dark goddess, any deed can be achieved.

Even Zeus, the father of the gods, fell under the spell of Hecate. He was known to direct all the immortals of his divine kingdom in what they were to do in the land of mortals. Only Hecate had no limits in her ability to grant or withhold the deepest desires in the hearts of mortals.

Some say that they who have Hecate's hidden knowledge may be granted all they wish if they would dare invoke her power: On the night of the dark Moon, go at midnight to a place where three roads meet. There in the darkness will the shadow form of the goddess be waiting. If you are gifted with eyes that see and ears that hear, she will teach you her hidden mysteries.

Lilith
ANCIENT SUMERIA

More than any other lunar deity, Lilith represents the alluring aspect apparent in the Moon. Lilith is the great seductress and ultimate temptress; she is dark passion and lust.

Like many Moon goddesses, Lilith is the most radiant of all beings, mortal or divine. She has one characteristic, however, that is hers alone. Her feet are depicted as giant claws, like those of a huge bird of prey. The claws mar her unearthly beauty and give her a demonic appearance.

In the case of Lilith, a demonic look is appropriate. According to the legends about her, she was Adam's first wife before Eve was given as his mate. The story is told that as Adam lay sleeping one night, Lilith lay down beside him and was united with him in his dreams. As a result of her trickery, Lilith became the mother of all the races of invisible beings that share the earth with humans. She is the mother of those we know as the faery folk and the spirits of the elements.

The Jews regarded Lilith as the Queen of Darkness. She reigned over all the spirits of evil intent. To ward off her power, the Jews wore amulets against her.

Like Hecate, her Greek counterpart, Lilith is the patroness of witchcraft and the goddess of the dark Moon. Her reign, however, takes a more malevolent tone. She is the dark enchantress, the evil queen of all sorcery.

Although Lilith pre-dates the Christian era, she was adapted into Christian legend when the new religion emerged. Her name is recognized as the consort of the devil. Lilith is thought to have twelve daughters, which represent the twelve fevers that plague the world.

Lilith is the goddess to whom requests are directed in many of the old European spells. She is the personification of all the erotic dreams and fantasies that come to plague people in the dark of night. She is the suppressed desires to taste the forbidden fruits of illicit love, to pursue lust for nought but its own sake, and to venture into the arena of debauchery and perversion.

In modern times Lilith is bonded with Christianity (one of the newest of the world's religions). Her worship, however, can be traced to a period far before the Christian church's emergence. One of the earliest representations of Lilith has been traced to ancient Sumeria in the year 2000 B.C.

While many of the beneficial Moon gods and goddesses of old have been assigned traits of negative quality by succeeding religions, Lilith has been relatively free from the hands of meddling newcomers. Because she was known already as a dark goddess, outsiders could do little to taint her reputation in the eyes of those who gave her worship.

Ancient Sumeria, however, has long faded from all but the history books. Those who knew Lilith at the height of her reign have perished centuries ago. Like the culture she served, Lilith, in her original form, survives as little more than a memory of days gone by.

Khons, the Forgotten Egyptian

The names of Ra, Osiris, Isis, Thoth, Horus, and Bast are among the Egyptian divine hierarchy that has out-lived the ancient culture of Egypt itself. These names are still spoken even though many centuries have passed since ancient Egypt's great civilization reigned. Few, however, remember the god Khons. In his day, he was numbered among the highest of the divine realm.

Originally, Khons was a Moon god. In time, howev-er, the reputation of Khons as a great healer became

more important than his role as a lunar deity; the popular pair of Thoth and Isis rose to rule the Moon and replace him.

One of the surviving tales concerning Khons unfolds during the reign of Pharaoh Ramesses.

It happened that in the twenty-third year of Ramesses' reign, a messenger from the Prince of Bakhtan arrived, bearing precious gifts for the Pharaoh's royal wife. When the messenger was admitted to the royal audience chamber, he bowed respectfully before Ramesses. "Great Lord," the messenger began, "my master, the Prince of Bakhtan, sends me not only with these gifts, but also with an urgent request for aid. Bentresh, the younger sister of your wife, Neferure, has been taken by a most strange and serious sickness. Can your majesty send someone who might restore her to health?"

Without delay, Ramesses summoned Djehuty-em-heb, the royal scribe and the finest healer in all of Egypt. Ramesses directed Djehuty-em-heb to accompany the messenger on his return to the prince's land.

As soon as he reached Bakhtan, the scribe examined Bentresh. When the examination was completed, he announced that the princess' illness had been caused by a spirit's possession. He felt that this spirit had such power that his own efforts would be futile. When the prince heard Djehuty-em-heb's diagnosis, he once again dispatched a messenger to the Pharaoh.

Upon hearing of his healer's failure, Ramesses went to the temple of Khons. He stood before the god's image and said, "I speak to you about the illness of

Bentresh. If you would but grant us your favour, the life of the girl might be saved." The image nodded to the Pharaoh to indicate his agreement and immediately set off for Bakhtan.

Upon the image's arrival, the people took Khons to the chamber of the ailing Bentresh. The god moved to the bed where Bentresh lay and passed his magical essence into her. The noise that issued from the princess' chamber was most terrifying, but when the door was opened, the girl was restored to health. Before the image of the god, the evil spirit that had possessed Bentresh lay prostrate.

A great celebration was held in honour of the healing god. All the people of Bakhtan were moved to great love for Khons and gave themselves over to rejoicing in his name.

No one's love for Khons was greater than that of the prince himself. It was the depth of his love for the god that stirred the prince to delay Khon's journey back to Egypt. In this, he succeeded for three years and nine months. One day, however, the prince had a vivid dream. He saw the god in the form of a golden falcon emerge from the shrine in which he lived. The golden bird rose high into the heavens and turned his course toward the land that was his home. When the prince awoke, he had a great feeling of guilt. He knew that his dream meant that the god wished no further delay in his journey home.

The prince made ready all the arrangements for Khons' return to Egypt. The people of Bakhtan who had come to love the god stood by him to bid farewell and shower him with fine gifts. When he returned to his native Egypt, Khons was happily restored to his own temple.

So ends a tale of the once-loved, too often forgotten Egyptian, the Moon god Khons.

Caridwen, Queen of the Cauldron
WALES

As it is with many lunar deities, the Celtic goddess Caridwen reflects the Moon's rule over life and immortality.

One of the greatest mythological treasures of Great Britain is Amen, the enchanted cauldron of Caridwen. The goddess used this vessel to brew the elixir of inspiration and science, which was known as *grael*. The same vessel later became popularized through the legends of King Arthur as the Holy Grail. Amen is also remembered as the cauldron of rebirth.

The most famous Caridwen legend is the story of making the grael. As it is recounted in the *Mabinogian,* the Welsh book of legends, the tale begins with the goddess' concern over the future welfare of her children.

Caridwen bore two children. The daughter, Creirwy, was the fairest maiden in all the world. The son, Avagddu, was not gifted with this same beauty. Avagddu was cursed with an ugliness beyond compare. Caridwen feared that her son would never be given the acceptance of nobles by reason of his great ugliness. "Perhaps if he had some other great virtues," thought the goddess, "his ill-favoured countenance might be overlooked." Thus it was that Caridwen began to boil a cauldron of inspiration and science for her son, as it is set down in the magical books of Fferyllt.

Once the potion was begun, it had to be kept boiling for the whole of a lunar year and a day. After this time had passed, three drops of the brew were taken to obtain the grace of inspiration.

Gwion Bach was set to stir the brew for the time of its brewing and a blind man named Morda was charged to kindle a fire and keep it hot so that the cauldron was kept bubbling the whole time. Every day, Caridwen gathered the proper herbs at the proper times and placed them into the cauldron.

Toward the end of the year, the goddess was out culling herbs while Gwion and Morda tended to the boiling cauldron. It happened that three drops of the magic brew flew out of the cauldron and landed on Gwion's fingers. He thrust his hand into his mouth to still the burning of the boiling brew and was immediately blessed with inspiration from the enchanted potion.

All at once, Gwion saw what was to be in the future. He knew that his greatest care would be to guard against Caridwen's wrath. Her anger would be intense when she learned that Gwion had received the inspiration intended for her son.

Gwion fled in fear of the goddess. When Caridwen returned, she saw the cauldron burst in two, for all the potion was most vile save for the three charmed drops of inspiration. She saw the year's work lost and became enraged. In anger, she pursued the fleeing Gwion. He took the form of a hare, and she a greyhound. He turned into a fish, and she pursued him as an otter. Gwion took to the air as a bird. Caridwen began to close in on him as a hawk. From the air, Gwion saw a pile of grain. In a last desperate move, Gwion turned himself into a single grain and hid in the pile. Caridwen assumed the form of a black hen and with her feet scratched at the pile of grain and found Gwion. The black hen swallowed the wheat. In nine months, he was reborn as Talesin.

Because of the child's great beauty, Caridwen's anger was softened. She could not bring herself to kill him. He grew to be one of the greatest Welsh bards.

○ ○ ○

In this legend, the same cauldron gives both life eternal and inspiration. The ceremonies that accompany the appointment of a bard or Druid parallel the legend of the magic cauldron of Caridwen. And, of course, a rite of initiation is considered to be a ritual of rebirth.

In early Celtic myth, the enchanted cauldron of Caridwen was used to restore slain warriors. Eventually, the cauldron was stolen away to the underworld, called the Land of Youth. There it remains as a clue to humans as to where they may find the key to immortality. The method of obtaining the key is also safe within the cauldron. If this insight is to be gained, it is through a gift of inspiration.

Caridwen still reigns in her nightly station as the Moon. Her cauldron is still a prize of the greatest value. A human can go on no greater quest than that of the search for truth. And the noblest of all truths lies deep in the cauldron of Caridwen.

Danu, the Good Mother

IRELAND

The ancient Irish people worshipped Danu, one of the earliest goddesses on the emerald isle. She was the dual goddess of the Tuatha de Danaan, or the people of Danu.

In one of her aspects, Danu has a beneficent nature. She is equated with Buan-ann, another early deity of Ireland, whose name translates to Good Mother. In this aspect, Danu is also known as Anu, worshipped as the Goddess of Plenty in Munster. Two fertile hills in County Kerry still bear her name; they are known as the Paps of Ana. The beneficent Danu is remembered as a Moon Goddess who oversaw the fertility of crops and cattle. She was the mother of Brian, Iuchair, and Iuchbar, the three Celtic culture heroes who captured the mythical treasures of the Tuatha de Danaan. The goddess nursed her sons so well that the word *Ana* came to mean *plenty* in her honour. Danu, in this aspect, is also known for the sweetness of the heather. It was she, according to legend, who gave the heather its aroma.

Danu is also remembered in her less positive, more hellish aspect. She is the great queen who can be seen in her dark aspect as the triad of Ana, Badb, and Macha. In this triad, Danu is the hag, the Goddess of the Moon in its dark phase. The folklore of Great Britain has preserved the goddess' malevolent nature; she is known as Black Annis of Leicester. The goddess kept a place in the Dane Hills where she devoured small children for her evening meal. After she had eaten her fill, she hung the children's skins on the boughs of an oak tree to dry.

The festivals held in Danu's honour were the fire festival of midsummer and of May eve. The midsummer fires were kindled in honour of Danu in her full Moon aspect, her benevolent character. May eve celebrations were dedicated to the hag. At this time, however, the goddess' dark nature underwent a transition, for there was a rite of love, the traditional love chase in her honour. For this particular feast, the hag seems to soften and take on the character of maidenhood.

In the early Christian days Danu, like many of the other ancient goddesses, became adapted by the clergy so as not to interfere with the church's supremacy in the mind and heart of the average peasant. Danu was, however, not afforded the prestige of canonization as were many of her sister goddesses. A legend was built up around the goddess that stripped her of her divinity and made her subject to the rule of the church. It is a story told along the Irish shores. It is the tale of an evil hag from Berle who became a nun and gave up her ways to follow the church. This hag is the dark aspect of Danu.

In tracing Danu's history, it becomes apparent that she is one of the most ancient goddesses. Some scholars believe she is the same divine personage as Danuna, an Aegean mother goddess of about 1200 B.C. She is also equated with Danae of Argos who reigned in about 2000 B.C. In any case, Danu is recorded to have come to Ireland with the Tuatha de Danaan in 1274 B.C. It is from that time that Danu, as a separate deity, began her reign as an Irish goddess.

Many legends exist about this Irish Moon Goddess. One of the best remembered tales credits her with the great deluge in Celtic mythology.

○ ○ ○

Danu (in an aspect known as Buan-an) was the keeper of an enchanted river. Her waters were the home of the salmon of all knowledge. Anyone who ate the flesh of the charmed fish would be given the gift of divine inspiration.

One day, the goddess caused the magic waters to overflow. All of Ireland was covered by the flood and all life was destroyed. Four survivors—Bith; his wife, Birren; a daughter named Cesara; and her husband,

Fintaan—sought to escape the flooded land. When it seemed that their safety was ensured, however, the Moon Goddess appeared big and red in the sky, surrounded by hundreds of clouds. These clouds expanded and broke apart. The survivors were not to endure the shower of cloud parts. The land was left uninhabited and free for the children of the goddess, the Tuatha de Danaan, to settle. The magic river of the goddess is still remembered in Ireland today and still flows. It is the River Boyne.

Danu was later changed to the masculine spelling *Don* with the emergence of patriarchal cultures in Ireland. As Don, she survived until the loss of her divinity and ultimate retreat to obscurity. None can deny, however, that it was Danu and no other who brought civilization to Ireland with her first great bronze age people, the Tuatha de Danaan, the children of Danu.

Isis, Mistress of Magic
ANCIENT EGYPT

Like many of the other lunar deities, the Moon goddess of Egypt is an enchantress. In the legends of Isis, her magic is boundless. No magician or sorceress the world has ever known would challenge the highest magic. It was only Isis, whose magic was so great, who would dare challenge the power of the creator of the universe.

As the ancients have recorded it, Ra was the creator of the land and sky. All humans, creatures, and even the

gods were of his making. Ra was the all-powerful king of both mortal and divine; everything was within his power. His forms were many, and he had as many names as he did faces. Some of his names were so secret that they were hidden even from the knowledge of the gods.

Isis became jealous at the great power of the father god. She began to consider how she might have the power of Ra for her own and become the mighty queen over the earth and heavens. After much thought, Isis came to the realization that there was but one way for her to claim dominion over the mighty Ra. If she could learn his most secret name, she would hold supremacy over his great power.

Isis formed a serpent out of clay and laid it down at the crossroads where she knew Ra came riding each day. There the serpent lay lifeless. At the arrival of Ra, however, the serpent became inspired by Isis' incantations and sprang to life. The serpent sank his fangs deep into the god and let his poison flow generously. Ra let out a mighty howl that filled the heavens and was overcome by weakness as the venom took over his body.

For a long time, the greatest of the gods lay helpless. His pain was constant. His weakness was growing. He no longer seemed the image of the universe's master. He was a figure to be pitied in his misery.

When the divine children of Ra heard that he was on his deathbed, they came quickly from all corners of the universe to be at his side. Ra summoned his remaining bit of strength and told them what fate had befallen him. When his tale was done, Isis, who had come equipped with her magic, spoke to him. Surely the right spell would drive away the evil and restore the mighty Ra to health.

Isis offered to breathe the air of life back into the father god, if he would reveal his most secret name to her. Ra hesitated to speak this name. He knew that whoever had this word of power could control the universe. In the end, however, he relented. The poison in his body was draining the last bit of life out of him. If he did not submit to the request of Isis, he would surely die. Ra warned the goddess that she must never repeat the secret name to any but her son Horus. He then spoke the word of power.

Isis made no hesitation in working her magic. In a short time, her work was done and Ra was completely restored. However, it was no longer Ra that was the master of the universe. Armed with the magic of the secret name, Isis now held dominion over all.

○ ○ ○

Perhaps Isis' courage and confidence, which she displays in her legends, account for the goddess' long endurance. While many of the other ancient divinities have been forgotten, the name of Isis lives on. Even in a society that has largely forgotten the religions of ancient times, Isis has become a patron goddess for women everywhere.

In these times when many women rise up against centuries of male domination, Isis is an inspiration. Perhaps the women of the new age can rise above the traditional rule of men, even as Isis gained dominion over Ra. Perhaps the men of today, inspired by the Egyptian goddess, will extend a hand to women that they might rule the world hand in hand, side by side.

The men of today remember the Egyptian enchantress. As is true of many of the ancient goddesses, the magic of Isis was not only in her spells and incantations but also in her unmatched beauty. In *The Golden Ass*, Apuleius described the vision of Isis as a woman with a "...face so lovely that the gods themselves would have fallen down in adoration of it."

Whatever the reason for her enduring allure, the reign of the Egyptian goddess has never quite ended. Even men of learning and science cannot help but be enchanted by the mistress of magic, the Goddess of the Moon, Queen Isis.

PART 3:
More
Moon Tales

A Sampling of Tales

Humanity has devoted more time to the Moon, and dedicated more legendry, than there is space for in a single volume of lore. In parts one and two, the Moon legends honoured deities that cultures had come to associate with the Moon.

Other Moon tales are neither rooted in survival nor religion but are lessons of everyday life. Some suggest a certain moral code or warn against certain cultural taboos while others seem to have no purpose other than to entertain. The tales that comprise this part are a sampling of many types of Moon tales.

Sitting on the Moon

Many cultures have regarded the Moon as a divine symbol and believed that its spirit ensouled the epitome of spiritual beauty and wisdom. Some traditions of Welsh descent have told a legend that reflects this belief.

One evening, as a young god was sitting on the Moon, he leaned over to take hold of the Moon's Western horn and look upon the earth. He could see that creatures filled the hills and valleys of the countryside. The Moon rode lower in the sky so that the god might be able to get a closer look.

Against the Eastern horn, the young god saw a Shining One, laying motionless in her place and setting her soft gaze upon the god. He saw the wisdom in the Shining One's gaze.

"Who are they who dwell in these lands below us?" the god asked.

"They are the women and men of the earth; the sons and daughters of The Infinite One," replied the Shining One in a soft voice of sweetest song.

The god looked again and saw that these creatures pushed, shoved, and thrashed their arms at each other as they hurried along their ways. If one of their fellow creatures lost his footing and stumbled, no one seemed to notice. The unfortunate one was trampled beneath them. When at last the creature's cries were heard, the few who bothered to stop did nought but kick him brutally.

Upon seeing this, the god became confused. Certain that he had misunderstood, he asked again, "Are they all the children of The Infinite One?"

"All," the Shining One answered simply.

Seeking some spark of comprehension, once more the god turned his gaze to the scene below. In time, it became clear to him that these creatures were in search of something. Because of this most frenzied search, they had become insensitive to any who hindered them along their path. That which they sought surely must be of great value to go to such great extremes in its quest. The young god felt compelled to discover more.

"What is it they seek with such singleness of purpose?" he asked the Shining One.

"Happiness," was her reply.

"Do they all seek happiness?"

Again, she answered simply, "All."

Suddenly, the god found himself taken by tears. He noticed a young woman who found a first love in a man whose eyes were fixed on a translucent stone of the deepest red hue. Without a word, the man cast the woman aside and reached for this glittering orb which, the god assumed, the man believed to contain happiness.

Knowing with what vigour they follow their paths, the god knew at once that there could be no end to the pain and suffering of these troubled creatures until at long last their goal was realized.

The god turned to the Shining One and asked, "Will they find the happiness which they so steadfastly seek?"

"They will find it," she replied.

"All of them?" he asked.

"All."

"Those who are trampled?"

"They will find it."

"And those who trample?"

"All."

The young god looked once more at the sad world below. After a long contemplation, he asked, "This search for happiness—is it the will of the gods or the twisted games of some foul demon?"

"It is the gods' will."

His heart still torn from the vision below, he asked, "But why must they ever pursue this happiness when it causes such misery?"

The Shining One replied, "They are learning."

"What is it that they must learn at such a price?" the young god asked, still confused.

And the Shining One replied, "They are learning life, and they are learning love."

The god was silent as he let the last words of the Shining One slowly drift within the grasp of his understanding. Then his attention was caught by a figure below. The bodies of struggling men and women were cast before this individual so that the path of his journey might be carpeted by their flesh. Full of pride, this man boldly walked over them, never once casting his eyes down to their pained and anguished faces. Suddenly, a whirlwind lifted this solitary figure and placed him down in another place, tearing his robes in the process. In the new place, he found himself naked among strangers, who descended upon him and brutally beat and mistreated him.

Pleased at finding that justice did have its place amid all the misery below, the god turned to the Shining One. "The man got what he deserved," he said.

The Shining One turned to the god and, with no sign of approval or disapproval, said, "As do they all. What each of them deserves is that which shall show them the way to true happiness."

As he pondered the meaning of these last words, the god kept studying the affairs of the world beneath him. As he did, however, a curious feeling overtook him. The god found that he could no longer feel pity only for those who were the objects of the cruelty below; he now felt pity for those who committed these grave acts. Still in search of answers, the god again turned to the Shining One.

"It is as if they are goaded into this life of insensitivity," he said. "Who goads them?"

Her reply was, "It is that which we call desire."

At first, the god thought desire to be the root of all that is painful. He almost raised his voice in protest but caught hold of himself and so was still. A thought struck the god that he could not ignore.

"Is it this desire that prompts these creatures to learn the lessons that are given by the gods?" he asked.

"It is," the Shining One answered.

"The lessons of life and love?"

"It is," she said.

No longer could the god see the people's actions as cruel. He saw only a group of lost individuals who were taking their first steps toward learning life's lessons. He continued to watch and felt a great compassion for those below. Now and then, a mighty wind would come to carry one or another of them away to continue learning in another place. This the god watched with a great fascination. He looked in awe upon the Shining One who inhabits the Moon. She who has watched over the earth for untold ages must know true compassion and understanding. His being drank its fill of her radiant countenance, and he knew her love as his own.

Diana's Moon Children

The magnificence of Ancient Rome emerged to bring all people together in the name of the mighty Empire. From the heart of the Roman giant comes the tale of the children of the Moon Goddess.

There once was a young man who lived just outside the great city of Rome. He was a man of little fortune, a wanderer. He had been alone in the world, without father or mother, for as long as he could remember. His life was hard and difficult; he often found himself

hungry and sorrowful. A happy soul, he was not. Yet he was a good man.

When the hardships of his life became too much to bear, he sought the solitude of a lonely place in the hills. There he sat for hours soothing his troubles and finding comfort in the shimmering Moon that rose above the hills.

One night, he lay upon the green grass in his secret place away from all the troubles of the world. He gazed at the land around him, lit softly by the Moon in its fullest light. The beauty of this land of nighttime splendour aroused within him the most delightful feelings of wonder mixed with serenity.

The man knew that the enchantment of this most lovely scene must be the work of the Moon, which had charmed people since the beginning of time. He lifted his eyes to the heavens so he might see the mysterious maid of the night—and was startled by what he saw.

There on the moonbeams danced a thousand small angels, winged and adorned with a glowing light that shone as silver as the Moon on high.

"What are you?" he asked, his eyes fairly starting out of his head.

A strange melodic sound, as the strings of a lute carried softly on the wind, quietly gave him his reply:

> *We are the children of the goddess,*
> *Whose moon shines through the night.*
> *Moon-rays. Moon-beams.*
> *Children of her light.*

We are the Faery Folk,
That rise when day is done.
Each ray the Lady Moon does send,
A Faery does become.

"Gladly would I be as you, O creatures of the night," remarked the youth. "No need of food or drink and never a care to put an end to your glorious dance."

"But you, too, are of our blood," the Faeries replied. "At the time you entered this world from the one that lies beyond, our Lady's Moon watched above in her fullest glory. Who is born in such a moment is favoured by the heart of the goddess and, like us, is a child of the night. We are of one spirit and of one heart, bound together by the love of the goddess of the Moon."

The youth joined in the dance of the Faery Folk and revelled through the night. When the light of the dawn began to break above the eastern horizon, he saluted the Moon of the goddess with a kiss and said his farewells to his newfound family.

The youth began his descent from the hills, still taken by the wonder of the night. He pondered the sorrow that had first beckoned him to the lonely hills. In an instant, he knew that his troubles were never to return again. Though others may have more money than they can count and lay a table that could feed great multitudes of the poor, they could never hope to match his wealth. He had the goddess' favour with him always and was as one with the magical race of Faery.

A Nigerian Moon Tale

Many people believe that when a man and woman lie down together in love, the children of the earth are conceived. The wise ones of the Nigerian tribes scoff at this idea. They know that a child would never emerge from the womb if not for the grace of the Moon.

In the earliest times, before the hunting spear was given to the world, the first man and the first woman lived happily in the village called paradise. Man went into the jungle each day and hunted with sharp stones so that the food he found might keep their bodies from hunger. The first woman remained in the village and spent her days sounding out nice rhythms against a tree with her pounding stick.

Each day was much the same. As the sun climbed higher in the sky, man gathered stones and began the hunting expedition. Woman took up her pounding stick and practiced her steady rhythms at her favourite tree. When man returned from his daily quest, the two ate their meal together. When their meal was done, woman showed man the new rhythms she had learned. She steadily beat them out for his entertainment.

This happy scene continued for many years; man and woman wanted for nothing. All that lay within the village and the land surrounding it was at their disposal. No need went unfulfilled.

At the time they were placed in the paradise, the creators had told man and woman, "No need shall there be that is not met. In the beauty of simplicity, you will live happily through the rise and set of every sun. Your purpose will not be more than to be joyful and to be fulfilled. Love each other well and care for each other's wants, and each day here will hold the same. Be always good to one another and gaze not upon the light that shines when the world is in slumber through the night. To do so will surely enrage us, and our wrath will soon be upon you."

One night, however, as man and woman lay sleeping after the light of day had fallen from its place in the sky, a strange sound awakened woman. Unable to return to her sleep, she arose from the place where she was resting. She was restless and began to think of the monotony of her days. She longed to have some kind of change. She remembered the words of the creators and began to wonder about the sun of the night. She knew it must be visible just above or beyond the cluster of trees where she lay each night to rest.

The warning of the creators ran over and over through her head. She knew the creators had forbidden her to look upon the light of night, but she so craved relief from her restlessness.

Woman hid herself behind some bushes that she had plucked from the earth in the hopes that she would not be seen by those who were her creators. With this disguise, she quietly set out to look for the night sun. Woman cast her gaze upward and beheld a beautiful ball of the most wondrous silver light. She was very much in awe of the forbidden sight's splendour and stood looking at it for a much longer time than she had intended. A nagging fear of discovery finally loosened her eyes from this sight, and she made her way back to the side of man. There she lay down very carefully, without making the slightest sound.

When daylight arose, man went off to seek his nourishment, and woman went back to pounding her rhythms. When she was certain that man was well out of sight, woman stopped her beating of rhythms for a moment and smiled knowingly to herself. How clever she was to conceal herself behind the bushes, she thought to herself. Even the creators must not have seen her!

Time went on, and each night woman woke from her slumber and gazed upon the light that was forbidden. Each time, she took up the bushes and concealed herself ever so carefully. She was sure that neither man nor the creators could ever discover her. She was soon to find she was mistaken.

One evening, when the sun was beginning its descent in the heavens, man emerged from the day of hunting. This day, however, he had nothing for their evening meal. He was tired from the long and unfruitful day and grew more irritable as his hunger increased. Woman knew that the creators' wrath must be upon them for her activities of the night. She feared that if man were to discover her nocturnal adventures, he would also become angered.

Woman tried to comfort man with the pounding of her rhythms. Each beat, however, only seemed to make him more upset. Finally, as the world began to darken, he could stand the noise no longer. He took the pounding stick from woman and, in his anger, he struck her with it.

They began to argue with one another. When her anger was at its height, woman lost control and let slip how stupid man was, that he lay sleeping each night unaware of her ventures. His rage at her nightly escapades was unbounded. Again and again he struck woman with the pounding stick. So great was his anger that he did not notice the sun of the night had risen in the sky above them. At the sight of it, he was astounded. He fell to the ground in awe of the vision.

It was then that they heard the night sun speak. "Man and Woman," it said, "be ashamed in your ways. You who are so fond of raising the pounding stick against another, let it be as part of you. Let it ever remind you that love is the way of the creators."

At these words, the pounding stick arose from the place where it had fallen and attached itself to man, just beneath his belly.

"Woman," the night sun continued, "you deny the creators that you may be with me. From this day forward, we will be as one. The blood of your body, as I rise and fall, will do the same. Your body will swell, even as mine grows big in increasing light.

"You who have forsaken innocence will not again know the ease of simplicity. In days to come, life will be difficult. The evening meal will not always be plentiful and will come only by the work of your own labours.

"In your time of punishment, however, I also give a gift of hope." Suddenly, a great bird was sent down from the sky and woman became great with child.

From that day, man and woman struggled to survive. The hunt was not always easy for man. Woman bore the pain of childbirth. From that day, children became the new hope.

Today, women of Nigeria who do not want to bear children keep themselves away from the Moon's light. They know that the moonbird flies on the Moon's silver rays.

Changing Woman

The Moon, known as Changing Woman, was born of the union of the mighty forces of Dawn and Darkness. Dawn was the father of Changing Woman and her mother was Darkness.

In the days of her youth, Changing Woman did not know her true parents. In the time of her youthful innocence, she looked to First Man and First Woman as father and mother.

The child was unlike other children of the world. She conversed with the voice of the Wind and soon

refused the food of her people so that she might find her sustenance by partaking of the sacred pollen.

One day, the wise Wind told Changing Woman of her true mother and father. Changing Woman, however, kept this knowledge to herself and quietly went about the business of growing up.

In twelve days, Changing Woman became the essence of maturity. She was fully developed and very wise. At this time, her first cycles of womanhood began and a Ceremony of Puberty was held for her. With the aid of Bridled Titmouse Woman and Marsh Wren Woman, First Man undertook the ritual and made offerings of White Shell and Turquoise. He pressed them to the body of Changing Woman, ritually uniting her with the Sun.

As time passed, Changing Woman grew discontent with First Man and First Woman and became quarrelsome. She remembered the secret knowledge the Wind had given to her. "You are not truly my mother," she told First Woman. "It is another who bore me. You had nothing to do with me."

Changing Woman separated herself from the lower world of First Man and First Woman. She journeyed to the west and built a dwelling place of her own, similar to the house of the Sun in the east. Her dwelling was well guarded and abundant in all the sacred stones of the Navajo people.

After she was settled in her home, Changing Woman bore twin children from her union with the Sun. These children became the hero models of the young Navajo boys who dream of becoming great warriors.

Changing Woman also gave life to the Holy People. At a meeting that the Navajo remember as the Blessing

Way, Changing Woman taught the Holy People how to control the Wind and the Storm and keep nature's forces in perfect balance and harmony. The Holy People, in turn, used this knowledge to create the universe, the earth, and a race called the Surface People, who we know as humans.

The Holy People formed the toes and fingernails of the Surface People from the abalone's shells. Their bones were made from white shell. Hair was created from darkness, the skull from dawn, and the brain from white shell. Sky waters were collected to form tears. The white of the eye was made from white shell, the pupils from mica and rock crystal, and earlobes and flesh were made from red-white stone. White shell beads provided the ability to hear. The nose was formed of abalone, and the teeth of white shell. The tongue was formed of lightning. Arms come from a rainbow; plants of every known variety were used to form the skin pores and pubic hair.

So it is, that but for the grace of Changing Woman, we would not be here upon the earth. The Navajo still look to the west with reverence where Changing Woman dwells in her beautiful house upon the waters.

A Man in the Moon

GERMANY

From the earliest days of youth, children are taught that they can look up at the night sky and see a marvelous wonder in the Moon. To the discerning eye, the bright Moon seems uninhabited. Little ones in many lands, however, can tell you with the greatest certainty that there is indeed a man in the Moon.

The legend of the man in the Moon survives throughout Europe in many different forms. Those who travelled to the Americas from the old world carried these tales across the Atlantic. Nursemaids in Germany still repeat the version below to those children in their charge.

Ages ago, on a bitterly cold Sunday in the winter season, an old man went to the woods to procure some sticks to burn in his fireplace. The wind was chilling as he made his way to the forest. He finally arrived at his destination and set about the task of hewing sticks. He worked quickly and soon cut as much wood as he was able to carry. He bound up these sticks into a faggot and slung it on a staff. He threw the staff over his shoulder and trudged homeward through the snow.

On his way, the old man met a handsome and youthful stranger. This fine young man was dressed in the most elegant Sunday attire and was walking toward the church. When he saw the old man with his bundle, the young man stopped. He turned to the elderly gentle-

man. "Old one," he said, "do you not realize that this day is Sunday upon the earth? It is the time when all people must take respite and put aside their labours."

"Sun-day upon the earth or Moon-day in the heavens," replied the old man. "It's all the same to me!"

"Then bear your burden forever," the stranger said. "And as you value not Sunday upon the earth, yours shall be a perpetual Moon-day in the heavens. You shall, for all eternity, stand upon the Moon. Let it be as a warning to any person who would honour not the Sabbath day."

Some say the stranger gave the old woodcutter a choice between burning in the fires of the sun or freezing in a lunar frost—and he chose the chill instead of the furnace. Others say the stranger suddenly vanished and the old man found himself instantly sitting upon the Moon.

How he got there is of little importance. The fact is that, to this day, if we look at the Moon when it is full, we can see the old woodcutter still carrying his faggot of sticks upon his shoulder. He has been there ever since that fateful day so many ages past.

When we take our rest upon the Sabbath, especially in the winter months, we can look out from the casements of our warm and comfortable houses and pity the sorrows of the old man who did not honour the day of rest upon the earth.

The Magic Pestle

BURMA

Today, people have grown used to the sight of the Moon in its progression across the sky each night. Many do not even notice her waxing and waning. Every school child knows of the earth's revolutions around the sun, and that the Moon is ever circulating about the earth. Tales of mystery and magic no longer abound. These days, science seems to be the greatest miracle. In Burma however, the elders still remember the ancient truths passed on to them by their grandfathers, and by the grandfathers before them. They know that the Moon did not always proceed across the sky, and they remember the way that it began.

Many years ago, an old woman lay in wait of the hand of Death. She had lived her life long and well and her time was ending, as it must end. Although she had been gifted with much happiness in her life, she had little material wealth. All that she had to leave to her grandson was a pestle.

When the old woman passed away, her young grandson took the pestle. He carried it always, for it was the only thing that he had to remember his beloved grandmother. The fact that it was all that she had to give made the pestle all the more valuable to the man.

One day the young man was walking in a field. As always, he had his pestle with him. On his walk he came upon a snake. When the snake saw the young man's pestle, he asked if he might borrow it for a short time.

"Why?" asked the young man. "Why would a snake have need of a pestle? It is of the greatest worth to me because it belonged to my grandmother whom I dearly loved, but of what possible value could it be to you?"

The puzzled young man listened attentively as the snake related a sad tale of how his beloved mate had died suddenly in the night. "I fear that I shall succumb to a death of loneliness without her," said the snake. "I ask the loan of the pestle that I may be able to restore her life to her."

The young man knew of no such magic in his pestle, but at the insistence of the sad reptile, he followed along to the lifeless body of the snake's beloved mate.

"If you please," said the snake, "touch the magic pestle to the nose of my beloved." Not knowing what else to do to relieve the snake's sorrow, the young man did as he was asked. When he did so, the lifeless body filled again with breath and the eyes of the dead snake opened.

"You could not have known," said the snake, "but your grandmother knew the magic of the ancient days. She befriended all that dwell in field and wood, and we too loved her dearly. Now that you know the secret of the pestle, you must guard it. If ever you speak the magic to another living soul, it will no longer work for you."

The young man took his leave of the snakes and headed back toward the village. He was filled with the wonder of the magic he had seen and tried to think how he might be able to use the gift of his grandmother for good. At the edge of the village, he came upon the lifeless body of a dog. The dog had died many days before and was beginning to decay. The man took out his pestle and touched it to the nose of the dog—the dog was alive again in an instant. Remembering the state of the dog when he had first come upon him, the young man called the dog Master Putrid and took him for his own pet.

In the days that followed, the young man and his magic pestle healed many people and brought many others back to life. In time, the king heard of the young man's ability and called upon his servants to find him. When his servants returned, a sorrowful king bade the young man to bring his daughter back from death with his magic. When the young man did this, the king rewarded the deed by giving the young man his daughter's hand in marriage.

The young man was happier than he had ever dared dream possible. He wanted his life with the princess to last forever. As he contemplated this pleasant prospect, he was struck by an idea. "If the magic that dwells within the pestle can bring life to the lifeless," he thought, "might it not give the youth of eternity if it is used on the quick?"

Taken by the possibility of holding to his happy life for all time, the young man was without delay in making his plans. On that very night after his wife had gone to sleep, he held the pestle to her nose and then to his own. Within a few weeks, it was evident that the magic pestle had given the gift of eternal youth.

It happened that the Moon had also seen the magic from her place high in the heavens. She was filled with jealousy by the magic she had witnessed. "All things must become aged and die," she said. "Even the sun of the day must fade at evening. It is not suitable that a mortal should command a power that even the sun cannot. I cannot allow such a thing to be. I will take the pestle from the youth!"

One day, when the young man had washed the pestle and put it out in the sun to dry, the Moon thought that she might have her chance to take it away. But it was not to be. All day the young man guarded his prize, and the Moon was unable to take it from him.

As the days passed, the young man's wife wanted her husband by her side all the time. She scolded him for being so overprotective of the pestle. Reluctantly, he heeded her words and came to her side. Still fearful for his pestle, however, he set his faithful dog, Master Putrid, to guard it. When the Moon saw that only a dog was left to ensure the magic pestle's safekeeping, she came down to steal it—and since it was still daylight, she was invisible. Master Putrid, however, smelled her strange scent as she neared, and he held himself alert. The Moon stole the pestle but could not escape the keen nose of Master Putrid. The dog began to follow her scent to retrieve the pestle.

The Moon can still be seen in her nightly course across the sky, trying to escape her canine pursuer. Sometimes, the dog catches his prey and we see a lunar eclipse. In the end, however, Master Putrid chokes because the Moon is too big for his throat. Then the eternal chase resumes.

That is the way that it all began, and so it must be until the end of time. Because the dog is always on the scent of the magic pestle, he is forever sniffing its youth-giving magic. He, in turn, is kept forever young and will never cease in the relentless pursuit of the Moon.

Moon Toads

NATIVE AMERICAN TRIBE AND CHINA

Many are the tales of the animals that have an intimate connection with the Moon. Although the hare is the most celebrated of the Moon beasts, another rather unseemly creature has its connection with the Moon as well: Some cultures' legendry insist that the toad abides in the lunar world.

Although his countenance commands no great appreciation in most people's eyes and his stature among the forest realm is not of the highest prestige, the toad has found a place in moonlore worthy of some attention. Among those peoples who hold the Moon toad in reverence are the Native American Selish people and the people of China. First, the legend of the Selish people.

The wolf had the greatest love for the toad. It was such an intense love that it swelled up within his heart and fairly consumed the wolf with passion.

One night, the wolf armed himself with the strength of his great desire and went in search of his beloved. This was the night he would court the toad and win her affections. Before he left, the wolf prayed to the Moon that she might shine brightly on his adventure. His prayer was answered and, beneath the bright light of a full Moon, the wolf set out to pursue the toad.

The toad saw the wolf in his search for her and managed to elude him for a long time. At last, the wolf saw by the clear moonlight that place in which the toad had taken refuge. The wolf stalked her in his quietest manner. When he was standing over the rock under which she had been hiding, he quickly turned over the rock and the bright moonlight enveloped her. It was then that the chase began!

The wolf pursued the toad throughout the night. The chase took them through swamp and wood, hill and meadow. Just as the wolf was about to close in on his love, she would jump her highest and farthest. In a moment, she would land again, far from his grasp. Then the chase was begun anew.

For several hours, they went on in this manner. The wolf would close in on the toad, and she would suddenly leap beyond his reach. But as time passed, the toad found it was more and more difficult to elude the wolf. The toad was growing weary. Her legs were growing tired and her leaps of escape did not carry her as far from the wolf as they had at first. As the night went on, her pursuer was getting closer to victory.

The toad knew that there was little power left in her legs. She had but one strong jump left within her. If she did not make it a good one, the wolf would surely be upon her. She was almost within the wolf's hold when she mustered all her strength and made her final attempt at freedom. With every bit of strength in her body, she made her last desperate and hopeful spring. When she landed, it was upon the face of the Moon. There she can still be seen when the Moon is full, far from the paws of the little wolf that would have her for his own.

In China, the story of the toad in the Moon is a different sort of legend. It does not concern the saga of an unlikely love, but tells of the drug of immortality.

Si Wang Mu possessed the magic elixir of life, the potion that could bestow the gift of eternal life on any who would drink it. The wife of this great magician was Chang-ngo. One day, Chang-ngo decided to steal the potion from her husband. As the magician slept, she took the vial that held his greatest magic. In the morning when the magician would discover the disappearance of his potion, his rage was certain to be great. Chang-ngo knew this and fled to the Moon to avoid his wrath.

Si Wang Mu arose with the sun the next day. When he saw that his wife was nowhere to be found, he became suspicious. He went to the chest where his potion of immortal life was kept. When he discovered it missing, his anger was even greater than his wife had imagined. He swore that he would find Chang-ngo, retrieve his potion, and kill her for her misdeed.

The magician used his powers to find Chang-ngo's hiding place and made no delay in carrying out his plans to secure the potion and deal with his thieving wife. Upon arriving on the Moon, Si Wang Mu found that his wife had consumed the elixir. He could neither make good his intention to retrieve the potion, for the vial was empty, nor deliver the punishment of death to the thief, for Chang-ngo was now immortal.

Now, Si Wang Mu was not to be diverted from his intention. He knew that his beautiful wife wanted to forever escape the ruinous hand of time. Now that she had taken the elixir, the wrinkles of age would never mar her beauty. The magician knew well the vanity of his wife and proceeded to use it against her in his revenge.

"You are wise to think, Chang-ngo, that no man may take your immortality from you now that you have taken the magic drug," said Si Wang Mu. "My power, as respected as it is, can be of little effect even against my own potion. In your haste to accomplish your purpose, however, I think you have forgotten your manners. You have not thought to have the courtesy to ask for the potion and have taken it without my knowledge. But if this is truly what you wish, dear wife, then it is what you shall have. If immortality is what you would have above all things, then tell me this is so and it will be yours with my blessing. I will make it yours by right and not merely by thievery."

Chang-ngo was surprised at the politeness, understanding, and peaceful manner of her husband. She was terrified of his bold power and most grateful that she did not have to endure his wrath. "Husband," she said, "your kindness makes me ashamed of my wrong against you. Life immortal is truly my wish above all things. I do wish it to be mine by right and not by deception."

"Then," said Si Wang Mu, "immortality is yours! But every magician has the right to ask payment for his services. If there is nothing more important to you in the world than immortality, whatever I ask will be but a meager reward for the gift that you've received. I take for my payment, your beauty." With that, Si Wang Mu turned Chang-ngo into a three-legged toad. She can yet be seen against the bright light of the Moon.

The Lake of the Moon

INDIA

Long ago, hares dwelt upon the shores of an enchanted lake called Candrasaras, or the Lake of the Moon. The sovereign king of all the hares had his palace upon the face of the bright Moon itself. Not far from the lake lived an elephant herd with their great monarch.

In this time, the rain had been especially scarce. Beneath the sun's heat, the earth became dry and cracked. The water holes became pits of dry sand. If water could not be found, the elephants knew they would die of thirst. They already found it difficult to

move their great bodies because of the weakness brought on by the increasing need for fresh water.

One day, one of the elephant scouts came upon the Lake of the Moon. Without delay, he hurried back to the herd to tell the elephant king of his discovery. Here was surely a place where the entire herd could still the pains of thirst. Here was a place to bathe in cool waters and take away the burning sting of the hot sun.

The elephant king gave the signal to assemble and march at once. In a short time, the herd had reached its destination at the shores of the lake. The elephants entered the water where they cooled their great bodies and stilled their parched throats.

Now the elephants did not know this, but all about the lake hare wardens protected the sacred waters from violation. When the wardens had seen the elephants approaching, they had managed to send most of the hares to shelter, but many were unable to get out of the herd's path. The feet of the marching elephants had killed or seriously injured many hares.

The elephants bathed to their hearts' content and satisfied their thirsty desires in the waters of the Moon. When they left, all was quiet again. The hares emerged from their places of concealment and helped their injured friends. Then they addressed the greater problem. They knew that the elephants would return and many more hares might be hurt in the stampede.

No simple answer could be found to the problem of the elephant herd. The hares could not order the elephants to stay away from the sacred lake. The hares knew the elephants would laugh at the small creatures.

Finally, one wise hare undertook the task of keeping

the elephants under control. He went to the king of all the herd and told him that he was the king of all the hares, the one who dwelt upon the Moon.

"It is my sacred mistress, the Moon herself, who sends me before you," said the hare. "If ever again you bring your herd to the sacred lake, you will bring her wrath upon you. From that day, the cool beams of night will be withheld and your bodies will be burned up by the relentless heat of a perpetual sun."

The elephant king knew that it was not a good idea to offend the Moon. His thoughts ran to ways that he might gain her favour once again. He offered to apologize for the offenses his herd had unwittingly committed against her. The Moon's self-appointed messenger accepted the offer.

When the king arrived at the edge of the sacred waters, he saw the reflection of the Moon. The Moon looked particularly solemn, thought the king, and must be planning her great punishment of the herd. Half out of fear, the elephant thrust his trunk in the water where the reflected moonlight stared back at him accusingly. When he realized what he had done, his fear was multiplied. Surely, the Moon's anger would be even greater now. Not knowing what else to do and certain that he had caused the Moon to become enraged by disturbing her reflection, the elephant king made quick his apology and ran back to his herd as fast as his great strong legs could carry him. He vowed never to return to the sacred lake again.

Epilogue

This book's original format was different from its current appearance. In completing the revisions and rewrites to the original work, I researched additional Moon legends. In my additional research, I found that moonlore has been a constant part of our daily lives throughout history.

A wealth of moonlore exists in the backgrounds of so many different cultures—it was more difficult to decide which tales to use rather than to find the appropriate material.

Perhaps its constant accessibility is the magic that has continued our fascination with the Moon. Its pale silver light entices the heart of people everywhere and caresses their soul.

I end this book with a saying from the sages of old:

> You can look but for an instant in the eye of the sun but
> all night upon the countenance of the Moon.

Appendices

Appendix 1

The Lunar Goddesses

Name	Nationality
Aataentsic	Iroquois
Anu	Celtic
Aphrodite	Greek
Aradia	Italian
Arianrhod	Welsh
Artemis	Greek
Ashtaroth	Phoenician
Astarte	Phoenician
Black Annis	Celtic
Brigantis	Celtic
Brigit	Celtic
Brizo	Greek
Caridwen	Welsh
Changing Woman	Navajo
Circe	Greek
Cybele	Greco-Roman
Danu (Dana)	Celtic
Demeter	Greek
Diana	Roman
Europa	Greek
Fana	Italian
Freya	Norse
Frigga	Germanic

Name	*Nationality*
Hathor	Egyptian
Hecate	Greek
Hera	Greek
Hina	Tahitian
Huythaca	Colombian
Inanna	Sumerian
Io	Greek
Ishtar	Babylonian
Isis	Egyptian
Juno	Roman
Lilith	Sumerian
Luna	Roman
Morgana	Celtic
Pe	African
Persephone	Greek
Sarasvati	Indian
Sedna	Inuit
Selene	Greek
Shing-Moo	Chinese

The Lunar Gods

Name	*Nationality*
Alako	Romany
Aningahk	Inuit
Chandra	Indian
Khons	Egyptian
Mani	Scandinavian
Maui	Polynesian
Metzli	Mexican
Nanna	Sumerian
Osirus	Egyptian
Ptah	Egyptian
Sinn	Babylonian
Somas	Greek
Tangaroa	Samoan
Tecciztecatl	Mexican
Thoth	Egyptian
Tsuki-yomi	Japanese

Appendix 3
Lunar Names

Saxon Moons

January	Wulf-Monat (Wolf Moon)
February	Mire-Monat (Softened Earth Moon)
March	Hraed-Monat (Stormy Moon)
April	Eastre-Monat (dedicated to Eastre, the Saxon goddess of rebirth and spring)
May	Preo-meolc-Monat (Three Milkings Moon)
June	Saer-Monat (Mild Weather Moon)
July	Maed-Monat (Meadow Moon)
August	Wyrt-Monat (Plant Moon)
September	Gust-Monat (Barley Moon)
October	Wyn-Monat (Wine Moon)
November	Blot-Monat (Blood Moon)
December	Yule-Monat (Yule Moon)

Osage Moons

January	Single Moon by Himself
	Frost on Inside of Lodge Moon
	Hunger Moon
February	Light of Day Returns Moon
March	Just Doing That Moon

April	Planting Moon
May	Little Flower Killer Moon
June	Buffalo Pawing Earth Moon
July	Buffalo Breeding Moon
August	Yellow Flower Moon
September	Deer Hiding Moon
October	Deer Breeding Moon
November	Coon Breeding Moon
December	Baby Bear Moon

Other Native North American Names

January

Big Manitou Moon, Snow Moon, Winter Moon, Old Moon, Moon of Frost in the Teepee, Cold Weather Moon, Ice Moon, Her Cold Moon, Hoop and Stick Game Moon, Man Moon, Trees Broken Moon, Younger Moon, Limbs of Trees Broken by Snow Moon, Moon When the Little Lizard's Tail Freezes Off, Play Moon.

February

Starving Moon, Storm Moon, Wind Moon, Running Season Moon, Frightened Moon, No Snows on Trail Moon, Exorcising Moon, Racoon's Rutting Season Moon, No Snow on the Road Moon, Trapper's Moon, Budding Time Moon, Elder Moon, Hunger Moon, Moon of Wind Scattering Leaves Over the Snow Crust, Moon When Coyotes Are Frightened, Moon of Dark Red Calves, Black Bear Moon.

March

Maple Sugar Moon, Lenten Moon, Sap Moon, Strong Wind Moon, Fish Moon, Worm Moon, Crow Moon, Chaste Moon, Moon of Snow-blindness, Moon of Wakening, Light Snow

Moon, Flower Time Moon, Seventh Moon, Lizard Moon, Cactus Blossom Moon, Little Wind Moon, All Leaf Split Moon, Moon When the Juice Drips from the Trees, Earth Cracks Moon.

April

Frog Moon, Sprouting Grass Moon, Egg Moon, Seed Moon, Eastern Moon, Pink Moon, Spring Moon, Moon of Grass Appearing, Do Nothing Moon, Wild Goose Moon, Deep Water Moon, Ashes Moon, Little Frogs Croak Moon, Moon of the New Grass, Eighth Moon, Leaf Spread Moon, Grease Wood Fence Moon, Big Wind Moon.

May

Planting Moon, Milk Moon, Mother's Moon, Hare Moon, Flower Moon, Moon When the Ice Goes Out of the Rivers, Ninth Moon, Moon When the Horses Get Fat, Corn Planting Moon, No Name Moon, Moon to Get Ready for Plowing and Planting, Moon When Ponies Shed, Salmonberry Bird Moon, Too Cold to Plant Moon.

June

Moon of Strawberries, Honey Moon, Moon of Making Fat, Hot Moon, Moon When the Buffalo Bulls are Rutting, Berry Ripening Season Moon, Rotten Moon, Turning Moon, Leaf Dark Moon, Hoeing Corn Moon, Hatching Moon, Turning Back Moon, Rose Moon.

July

Raspberry Moon, Hay Moon, Buck Moon, Mead Moon, Moon When Cherries Are Ripe, Moon of the Giant Cactus, Corn Tassel Moon, Ripe Moon, Thunder Moon, Rain Moon, Trees Broken Moon, Advance in a Body Moon, Whale Moon, Red Salmon Time Moon, Sun House Moon, Go Home Kachina Moon.

August

Mating Moon, Grain Moon, Dog's Day Moon, Woodcutter's Moon, Sturgeon Moon, Green Corn Moon, Wart Moon, Red Moon, Moon When Cherries Turn Black, Blackberry Patches Moon, Collect Food for the Winter Moon, Wheat Cut Moon, All the Elk Call Moon, Autumn Moon, Berries Ripen Even in the Night Moon, Chokeberry Moon, Summertime Moon, Moon of Spawning Salmon.

September

Hunting Moon, Fruit Moon, Dying Grass Moon, Barley Moon, Moon When the Calves Grow Hair, Cool Moon, Leaf Yellow Moon, All Ripe Moon, Corn in the Milk Moon, Moon Without a Name, Moon of Leaves Turning Colour, Moon of the Black Calves, Moon of Spiderwebs on the Ground, Big Feast Moon, Moon When Plums Are Scarlet, Moon of Wild Plums, Little Wind Moon.

October

Moon of Falling Leaves, Hunter's Moon, Moon When the Water Freezes, Blood Moon, Moon of the Changing Season, Her Leaves Moon, Travel in Canoes Moon, Great Sandstorm Moon, Leaf Fall Moon, Falling River Moon, Basket Moon, Moon of Freezing, Big Wind Moon.

November

Harvest Moon, Beaver Moon, Frosty Moon, Snow Moon, Autumn Time Moon, Every Buck Loses His Horns Moon, All Gathered Moon, Stomach Moon, Snowy Mountains in the Morning Moon, Initiate Moon, Corn Moon, Moon When Deer Shed Their Horns, Moon of the Falling Leaves.

December

Cold Moon, Christmas Moon, Moon Before Yule, Oak Moon, Moon of the Popping Trees, Her Winter Houses Moon, Long Night Moon, Christ's Moon, Night Moon, Cold Month Moon, Ashes Fire Moon, Turning Moon, Little Manitou Moon, Middle Winter Moon, Big Freezing Moon.

Author's Note: Many of the traditional names repeat in succeeding months. Because of people's tendency to reflect nature in the lunar names, the slight differences in seasons due to varying geographic location can alter the appropriate place for a lunar cycle. Growers in a warmer climate, for example, may harvest or plant at a later time than growers in a cooler one. The Harvest Moon, or Planting Moon, for one group may be in a later month for another group. Some cultures did not have names for every lunar cycle throughout the year. When necessary, the names were repeated, or "No Name Moon" was used.

Bibliography

Bellamy, H. S. *Moons, Myths, and Man.* Ann Arbor, MI: University Microfilms International, 1959.

Briggs, Katherine. *An Encyclopedia of Fairies.* New York: Pantheon Books, 1976.

Brueton, Diana. *Many Moons.* New York: Prentice Hall, 1991.

Cain, Kathleen. *Luna Myth and Mystery.* Boulder, CO: Johnson Printing, 1991.

Campbell, Joseph. *Myths to Live By.* New York: Bantam Books, 1972.

Curtis, Natalie. *The Indians' Book.* New York: Dover Publications, 1968.

Ellis, Peter Berresford. *Dictionary of Celtic Mythology.* New York: Oxford University Press, 1992.

Frazer, Sir James G. *The Golden Bough.* New York: Macmillan, 1922.

Gordon, Stewart. *The Encyclopedia of Myths and Legends.* London: Headline Book Publishing, 1993.

Graves, Robert. *The White Goddess.* New York: Farrar, Straus & Giroux, 1966.

Guest, Lady Charlotte. *The Mabinogian.* Chicago: Academy Press, 1977.

Guiley, Rosemary Ellen. *Moonscapes.* New York: Prentice Hall, 1991.

Hague, Michael. *Michael Hague's Favorite Hans Christian Andersen Fairy Tales.* New York: Holt, Rinehart and Winston, 1981.

Hamilton, Edith. *Mythology.* New York: New American Library, 1942.

Harley, Rev. Timothy. *Moon Lore.* London: Swann, Sonnenschein, Le Bas, & Lowery, 1885.

Hultkrantz, Ake. *The Religions of the American Indian.* Berkeley: University of California, 1967.

James, G. H. *Myths and Legends of Ancient Egypt.* Toronto: Bantam Books, 1971.

Leland, Charles G. *Aradia: Gospel of the Witches.* New York: Samuel Weiser, 1974.

MacKenzie, Donald A. *German Myths and Legends.* New York: Crown Publishers, 1985.

Nichols, Ross. *The Book of Druidry.* San Francisco: Aquarian Press, 1990.

Proctor, Mary. *Legends of the Sun and Moon.* London: George G. Harrup, 1926.

Rockwell, David. *Giving Voice to Bear.* Niwot, CO: Roberts Rinehart Publishers, 1991.

Stassinopoulos, Arianna, and Roloff Beny. *The Gods of Greece.* New York: Harry N. Abrams, 1983.

Thomas, Keith. *Religion and the Decline of Magic.* New York: Charles Scribner's Sons, 1971.

Van Over, Raymond. *Sun Songs: Creation Myths from Around the World.* New York: New American Library/Mentor, 1980.

Index

On the following pages you will find listed, with their current prices, some of the books now available on related subjects. Your book dealer stocks most of these and will stock new titles in the Llewellyn series as they become available. We urge your patronage.

To Get a Free Catalog

To obtain our full catalog, you are invited to write (see address below) for our bi-monthly news magazine/catalog *Llewellyn's New Worlds of Mind and Spirit*. A sample copy is free, and it will continue coming to you at no cost as long as you are an active mail customer. Or you may subscribe for just $10 in the United States and Canada ($20 overseas, first class mail). Many bookstores also have *New Worlds* available to their customers. Ask for it.

To Order Books and Tapes

If your bookstore does not carry the titles described on the following pages, you may order them directly from Llewellyn by sending the full price in U.S. funds, plus postage and handling (see below).

Credit card orders: VISA, MasterCard, American Express are accepted. Call us toll-free within the United States and Canada at 1-800-THE-MOON.

Special Group Discount: Because there is a great deal of interest in group discussion and study of the subject matter of this book, we offer a 20% quantity discount to group leaders or agents. Our Special Quantity Price for a minimum order of five copies of *Moonlore* is $51.80 cash-with-order. Include postage and handling charges noted below.

Postage and Handling: Include $4 postage and handling for orders $15 and under; $5 for orders *over* $15. There are no postage and handling charges for orders over $100. Postage and handling rates are subject to change. We ship UPS whenever possible within the continental United States; delivery is guaranteed. Please provide your street address as UPS does not deliver to P.O. boxes. Orders shipped to Alaska, Hawaii, Canada, Mexico, and Puerto Rico will be sent via first class mail. Allow 4–6 weeks for delivery. **International orders:** Airmail—add retail price of each book and $5 for each non-book item (audiotapes, etc.); Surface mail—add $1 per item.

Minnesota residents add 7% sales tax.

Mail orders to:
Llewellyn Worldwide, P.O. Box 64383-342-5
St. Paul, MN 55164-0383, U.S.A.

For customer service, call (612) 291-1970.

All prices subject to change without notice.

Moon Magick

MYTH & MAGIC, CRAFTS & RECIPES, RITUALS & SPELLS
BY D.J. CONWAY

No creature on this planet is unaffected by the power of the Moon. Its effects range from making us feel energetic or adventurous to tense and despondent. By putting Moon energy to work for you, you can learn to plan projects, work and travel at the optimum times.

Moon Magick explains how each of the 13 lunar months is connected with a different type of seasonal energy flow and provides modern rituals and spells for tapping this energy and celebrating the Moon phases. Each chapter describes new Pagan rituals—79 in all—related to that particular Moon, plus related Moon lore, ancient holidays, spells, meditations and suggestions for foods, drinks and decorations to accompany your Moon rituals. This book includes two thorough dictionaries of Moon deities and symbols.

By moving through the year according to the 13 lunar months, you can become more attuned to the seasons, the Earth and your inner self. *Moon Magic* will show you how to let your life flow with the power and rhythms of the Moon to benefit your physical, emotional and spiritual well-being.

1-56718-167-8, 7 x 10, 320 pp., illus., softbound $14.95

Lady of the Night

A HANDBOOK OF MOON MAGICK & RITUAL
BY EDAIN McCOY

Moon-centered ritual, a deeply woven thread in Pagan culture, is often confined to celebration of the full moon. Edain McCoy revitalizes the *full potential* of the lunar mysteries in this exclusive guide for Pagans who honor the Old Ways and seek new ways to celebrate the Lady who is always young.

Lady of the Night explores the lore, rituals, and unique magickal potential associated with *all* phases of the moon: full, waxing, waning, moonrise/moonset and dark/new phases. Combined with an in-depth look at moon magick and suggestions for creating moon rituals that address personal needs, this is a *complete* system for successfully riding the tides of lunar magick.

Written for both solitary and group practice, this book is exceedingly practical and versatile. *Lady of the Night* reveals the masculine side of the moon through history and breaks new ground by showing how both men and women can Draw Down the Moon for enhanced spirituality. Pagans will also find fun and spirited suggestions on how to make the mystery of the moon accessible to non-Pagan friends and family through creative party planning and popular folklore.

1-56178-660-2, 7 x 10, 240 pp., illus., softcover $14.95

Dark Moon Mysteries

WISDOM, POWER AND MAGICK OF THE SHADOW WORLD

BY TIMOTHY RODERICK

You are a blend of balancing energies: masculine and feminine, active and passive, and light and dark. However, most books on spirituality and empowerment avoid addressing your psyche's native darker aspects— even though it's vital that you claim your "darkness" to becoming a whole, integrated, empowered person.

Dark Moon Mysteries is the first book to explore the "dark side" of spirit, ritual, psyche, and magic. It is also the first book on Witchcraft to make use of storytelling to access wisdom and insight, in the tradition of *Women Who Run with the Wolves.* This book weaves together Jungian analysis, the practical application of imagery from ancient fairy tales, and contemporary Witchcraft to help you come to grips with the darker shades of your being. You'll use magic, rituals, dance, guided journeys, and more to explore your deep consciousness.

Work spiritually and magically with the Dark Moon to touch upon the very source of your inner power and to move beyond your fears and limitations. Embrace *all* aspects of your psyche and follow the *true* path of the Witch, shaman, magician and mystic.

1-56718-345-X, 6 x 9, 240 pp., illus., softcover $14.95

Maiden, Mother, Crone

THE MYTH AND REALITY OF THE TRIPLE GODDESS
BY D.J. CONWAY

The Triple Goddess is with every one of us each day of our lives. In our inner journeys toward spiritual evolution, each woman and man goes through the stages of Maiden (infant to puberty), Mother (adult and parent) and Crone (aging elder). *Maiden, Mother, Crone* is a guide to the myths and interpretations of the Great Goddess archetype and her three faces, so that we may better understand and more peacefully accept the cycle of birth and death.

Learning to interpret the symbolic language of the myths is important to spiritual growth, for the symbols are part of the map that guides each of us to the Divine Center. Through learning the true meaning of the ancient symbols, through facing the cycles of life, and by following the meditations and simple rituals provided in this book, women and men alike can translate these ancient teachings into personal revelations.

Not all goddesses can be conveniently divided into the clear aspects of Maiden, Mother and Crone. This book covers these as well, including the Fates, the Muses, Valkyries and others.

0-87542-171-7, 6 x 9, 240 pp., illus., softcover $12.95